30 Days to Your New Life

Other books by Anthony DeStefano
from Sophia Institute Press:

The Grumpy Old Ox

The Beggar and the Bluebird

The Seed Who Was Afraid to Be Planted

Joseph's Donkey

Our Lady's Wardrobe

Our Lady's Picture Book

How the Angels Got Their Wings

Anthony DeStefano

30 DAYS TO YOUR NEW LIFE

A Guide to Transforming Yourself from Head to Soul

SOPHIA INSTITUTE PRESS
Manchester, New Hampshire

Cover design by Mayfly Design.

Cover image (672916372) © Orla / Shutterstock.

Sophia Institute Press
Box 5284, Manchester, NH 03108
1-800-888-9344

www.SophiaInstitute.com

Sophia Institute Press® is a registered trademark of Sophia Institute.

paperback ISBN 978-1-64413-662-1

ebook ISBN 978-1-64413-663-8

Library of Congress Control Number: 2023931003

First printing

This book is dedicated with immense gratitude to
my late friend and literary manager,
Peter Miller

Contents

Week 3: Put Your Priorities in Order

Week 4: Start Your New Life

Reading Plan for This Book

The purpose of this book is simple but ambitious: to help you radically transform your life for the better in thirty days.

In order to achieve this objective, you must be willing to do a few things:

First, you have to have a thick skin. I won't be pulling any punches in this book. Life is too short. For this program to have any value, you've got to be willing to endure some straight talk. We don't have time to mince words or beat around the bush or be overly diplomatic. Of course I want to be compassionate, but sometimes the best way to do that is to tell the honest truth. I apologize in advance if you've been through any kind of intense suffering and this book seems too stern in its tone. It's not meant to be. It's meant to help decrease your suffering. So please bear with my "tough love" approach and stay the course.

Second, you must be an active reader, and not a passive one. It's so easy to read a book from cover to cover with enjoyment and yet get nothing practical out of it. That's fine if you're reading only for pleasure, but the purpose of this book is to impact your life in a significant way. Unless you take action in addition to merely reading words, there's virtually no chance that any real change will occur. To that end, I have included action items at the close of each chapter. I cannot emphasize enough how important it is for you to do them. They are there to give you greater clarity of purpose and, more importantly, to help you build momentum—momentum that will hopefully continue *after* you finish this book and for decades to come. Therefore, the first thing you need to do is buy a notebook or open a document on your computer or tablet devoted exclusively to these short assignments. Every day you'll be writing or typing your notes there, and it's very important to have them in one secure, private place so you can refer to them at the end of each week and at the end of the program itself.

As the book's title states, this is a 30-day program. Each chapter corresponds to one day of the program. Because of this, you should read only *one chapter per day*. Some of the chapters—especially those at the beginning—are short. That is by design. You might be tempted to skip ahead because you're a fast reader. Please don't! Instead, do the action items carefully, neatly, and perfectly, and then reread the same chapter—several times if necessary. I say again: do not skip ahead.

The book's 30-day program is divided into four weeks. Each week consists of six workdays and a seventh day devoted to rest. Even nonreligious readers will recognize that we are employing the same plan that God used when He created the universe. The reason is that we are trying to help you create a new *you*. Therefore, do not try to improve upon the book's plan. You can't do better than God.

Given the six-day workweek, it is essential that you start reading "Day 1" on a Monday. If you do that, your rest days will be on Sundays. This is absolutely necessary for maximum success, and as you go deeper into this program, you'll discover why. What this means is that, if you've purchased this book on a Tuesday, you should put it aside and wait until next Monday to begin reading it. It doesn't matter if you want to get started right away. Resist the temptation. Get through the week some other way. Read a good mystery novel. Watch your favorite TV series. Spend some quality time with your family. Best of all, get yourself to church and do some extra praying! Put yourself in the right frame of mind to receive and process all the truths that are contained in these pages. Trust me, it will be well worth the wait to start on the correct day.

That's all for now. Congratulations for taking this first step on the road to transforming your life. Hopefully you'll look back on it as a very important and meaningful moment in your life.

Now go get that notebook or computer file ready!

See you Monday!

Get Back to Basics

Wake Up!

Most people are asleep. They're born asleep, they live asleep, they marry asleep, they have children asleep, they grow old asleep, and they die asleep. They're just asleep—all the time. And the worst part of it is that they don't even realize it; they're completely oblivious to the fact that they're asleep. Most people today are not real, living human beings—they're walking zombies.

Everyone says they want to be happy. Everyone says they want to be fulfilled. Aren't you tired of hearing that? There are thousands of books, magazine articles, podcasts, YouTube videos, Internet memes, and television shows on the subject, and the whole personal-development industry is built on it. People today go around pursuing happiness as if it were something they could obtain or possess or achieve. They treat happiness as if it were some kind of shiny, colorful toy that's in the corner of the room, and all they have to do is go over and get it.

But that's not the way it works. And that's why people are asleep. They spend hundreds of hours trying to look younger, or become healthier, or improve their relationships, or pay their bills, or achieve financial freedom, or buy that Mercedes or that beach house, and a million other things, and when they finally accomplish their goal—*if* they accomplish their goal—they're *still* not satisfied. And they wonder why.

They're not happy because they're still asleep. They're still asleep—and even worse, they're having the same nightmare!

Remember Pinocchio, the little puppet who wanted to become a real boy? That's actually a very profound story because it has to do with the idea of free will and what it means to be an authentic human being. And it has deeply Christian undertones as well because it's all about how we have the power to become children of God and not just remain wooden, robotic marionettes. But do you know that today most of us are living the Pinocchio story *in reverse*? Instead of trying to become real, free, living human beings, we spend our lives trying to become puppets!

That's right. From the time we're born till the time we die, we continually attempt to attach "strings" to ourselves.

Some of these strings are material, such as those we attach to possessions, and some are immaterial, such as those we attach to places or activities or relationships. Some are good, such as those we attach to our families and friends, and some are bad, such as those we attach to status symbols and other vain pursuits. The point is not to judge the merit of these strings now. The point is simply to recognize that they exist. The fact is, we're always tying ourselves to things, and the result is that we have less freedom and less autonomy—not more. We actually *want* to make ourselves into puppets.

How do we do that?

You've heard the expression "Be careful about your possessions, or your possessions may end up possessing *you*." Well, that's what happens to many of us much of the time. Whenever you buy something or use something or rely on something to achieve happiness, an invisible string shoots out from that thing and attaches itself to your soul. Whether it's a car or a house or a watch or a job or a person or a place or a relationship, it always does the same thing: it exerts a claim on you. Always.

By the time you're a teenager, you've got hundreds of these strings coming out of you, attaching you to hundreds of objects—both animate and inanimate. And so you begin to live as a puppet. Your freedom to act in ways that are in accordance with your conscience or with the truth or with your deepest spiritual beliefs is so restricted that you really have no freedom at all. And even worse—you're oblivious to it. You're a puppet who doesn't even know you're a puppet. You're a sleeping puppet!

Again, don't mistake what I'm saying. I'm not asserting that all strings are negative. Some strings are positive. Some strings are necessary. Nor am I saying that all acquisitions are bad. I'm not ranting against "materialism" here. I'm not proclaiming any kind of gospel of poverty or saying that it's wrong to be rich. Yes, it's true that people are too materialistic, but that's not the point I'm making. Things can be good. Things can be fun. There's a place for them in life. But it's our priorities that are all screwed up. Instead of spending 90 percent of our time focusing on what will really make us happy, and 10 percent on the pursuit of things, people do the exact opposite. Everything we do and think is centered on obtaining money, houses, cars, clothes, gadgets, wine, women, and song. I once saw a framed poster that said: "In the game of life, whoever gets the most toys wins!" That's the spirit of the society in which we're living.

Nor am I saying here that your career and your health and your relationships aren't important. Of course they are. Of course it's important that you care deeply about them. I'm not saying that marriage or anything that ties you down to responsibility is bad because it limits your freedom. That's a million miles away from what I mean. What I'm simply trying to get across is the fact that *none of these things is going to make you happy*. None of them is going to give you true fulfillment. None of them is going to give you authentic freedom. None of them is going to give you lasting peace. It's all an illusion. It's all a big, fat lie.

These things all work for a while, and then they lose their power. The exhilaration you get from those trips to the gym, or from your lover, or from vacations, or from possessions, or from anything else that gives you pleasure or provides you with distractions or makes you feel fulfilled is just temporary. And eventually, when your health deteriorates, or you lose your job, or your kids grow up, or the person you're so in love with disappoints you or leaves you or dies, you're going to see clearly that it was all an illusion.

I'm telling you a simple fact. If you base your happiness on anything the world tells you is important—or on anything that may happen to feel good in the moment—you're going to end up being miserable. If you want to be happy, you have to completely forget about the world's standards of happiness. You have to shoot for something higher. C.S. Lewis said that if you aim for the earth, you will *not* get it; but if you aim for Heaven, you'll get Heaven and the earth thrown in too.

For goodness' sake, look around you! Look at all those people jogging and dieting and juicing and eating vitamins and using twenty kinds of skin cream. They're all trying to add a few years to their lives. Wonderful! God bless them! But even if what they're doing is effective—and that's debatable—what are they really gaining? If they do manage to live ten years longer, does it matter if those ten years are spent living as ignorant puppets? If those ten years are spent being fundamentally unhappy? If those ten years are spent being asleep? First wake up, and then worry about living longer!

The same goes for looking younger. The same goes for getting rich. The same goes for doing great at your job. The same goes for being a terrific parent. The same goes for "personal development" and "self-improvement." The same goes for finding the love of your life. You have to wake up first to really, truly, deeply, and *permanently* enjoy any of these things. You have to wake up and look at yourself and see all the thousands of strings you've got coming out of your soul, attaching you to a thousand things—some of them necessary, some of them good, some of them worthless, many of them bad, and *all* of them temporary.

Do you hear me? You've got to wake up first. Life is short. Do you understand that you could be dead by tonight? You could be hit by a car or shot in a robbery or have a stroke or a heart attack or a brain aneurysm within hours of closing this book. It's true. The same God who gave you the morning does not promise you the evening. Happiness is not about possessions. It's not about attachments. It's not about money. It's not about success. It's not about improvement. It's not even about human relationships. Those are all beautiful, but they're all secondary; they're all contingent; and the pleasure they bring is all dependent upon something else.

What is that something else?

That's the subject of this book.

Action Items

✓ Open your notebook or computer document and make a list of all the things in your life that you are attached to—i.e., all the things that you depend on for your well-being. Be sure to include any important relationships with people and pets, your job, your possessions, your hobbies, habits, compulsions, and addictions. Don't forget the world of technology and social media and sports. When you're finished, put asterisks next to your top ten attachments. Go through these top ten and label them as "good," "bad," or "neutral." Finally, underline any attachments that are particularly negative. We'll be addressing these later.

Get Off Your Pity-Pot!

There's only one place to start a book like this. And that's to say, without mincing words, that what you need to do right now is stop complaining!

If you're anything like me, you probably get a lot of pleasure from whining and moaning and complaining. It seems to be a common human trait. We don't have time now to do any amateur psychoanalyzing about why. It's just a fact of life. But it's time to stop. Right this very second!

If you're ever going to solve your problems—and I don't care what those problems happen to be—the first thing you have to do is get off your pity-pot.

Remember that scene from *The Godfather* when the Hollywood singer, Johnny Fontane, goes to Don Corleone and starts crying to him about all the terrible things that are happening in his life? He has no money. His marriage is breaking up. Nobody is buying his records. He can't get a job in the movies. And all he can do is whimper and weep like a little girl and ask over and over, "What am I gonna do? What am I gonna do?"

And do you remember what the Godfather does? Instead of sympathizing with him or showing him any compassion (as many of today's psychotherapists might be inclined to do), he stands up suddenly, grabs him by his jacket, starts shaking him furiously, and yells at the top of his lungs: "You can stop crying and *act like a man*!"

Well, it's time for you and me to follow that advice.

And if you happen to be a woman and don't want to "act like a man," then you can "put on your big-girl panties" instead—or use whatever other expression you like—as long as it helps you to stop wallowing in self-pity.

Yes, I know that self-pity is sometimes okay and even necessary. All my life I've listened to people complain—and all my life I've heard myself complain too. Sometimes we need to let it out. Sometimes we need to just wring our hands and bemoan our fate and cry out to Heaven: Why me?

But not all the time. And not for long. And certainly not when we *really* want to change things. Because when we really want to take control of our lives and turn things around, there is absolutely no place for self-pity or complaining. They're useless. Life is too short. It goes by in a flash—for everyone. You simply can't spend a lot of your time grumbling about your problems. Believe me, you'll regret it. So enough already. It's time to *do* something.

Have you ever heard of the "if only" syndrome? It occurs whenever we experience problems. Instead of being honest, we say to ourselves, "If only such-and-such were the case, then everything would be fine—then I could be happy." If only I made more money. If only I had a better job. If only I could lose weight. If only my wife were more appreciative. If only my husband were more romantic. If only, if only, if only.

But you know what? It's all garbage. It's all nonsense. If you miraculously got a million dollars right now, I'm sure you'd be very excited, and I'm sure you'd be able to pay off all your debt—for a while. But in about a year's time, I bet you'd have other money problems to deal with, or other family problems, or other emotional problems, or other health problems—and you still wouldn't be happy. You'd be saying "if only" about something else.

The problem isn't with the specific challenge you're facing—whether it's finances or relationships or whatever. The problem is with you. *You!* Admit it already. Take ownership for once! Stop lying to yourself. Wake up!

I'm not trying to be cruel. My point here isn't to make you feel guilty. It's to make you get honest with yourself. Remember, it's not just you. It's me, too. It's everyone—whether you're old or young, rich or poor, good or bad. We're all a bunch of crybabies. Some of the greatest saints in history have been guilty of this. In fact, sometimes the holiest people in the world have been the biggest, most annoying complainers.

Let's take an example from the Bible—the great St. Paul himself. He was an extraordinarily holy man, everyone agrees. But do you know something? He could be pretty annoying too. In fact, he was so annoying to the Romans that they eventually chopped his head off.

Well, just like you and me, St. Paul went through a version of the "if only" syndrome. In one of his famous letters, he talks about how God had given him some kind of "thorn" in his flesh to "torment" him and keep him humble. He never says exactly what the affliction was—it could have been anything: a bad temper, a physical problem, a spiritual temptation; who knows?—but he does say that he begged God three times to take it away from him. He basically did what we were describing a moment ago: he whined and complained to God.

But do you know what God did? He didn't console or sympathize with him in any way. Instead, He said: Enough! "My grace is sufficient for you, for my power is made perfect in weakness" (2

Cor. 12:9). In other words, God told him to shut up! And after that stern rebuke, Paul didn't complain anymore. In fact, he actually began to take pleasure in the hardships and persecutions he had to endure because he knew that somehow, some way, God was going to help him *more* when he was weak and suffering than when he was feeling strong.

And that's the same lesson we have to learn.

You see, over and against the noisy cacophony of human moaning and whining and complaining that has polluted the earth's atmosphere since time immemorial, there stands alone the simple and quiet figure of Jesus Christ. And Christ has one message for humanity, one message of "tough love" for all of us. And that message is this: Enough! "My grace is sufficient!"

So you're down-and-out and can't take it anymore? You're tired of problems. You're tired of bills. You're tired of fighting with your spouse and with your kids. You're tired of being misunderstood. You feel that you're at the end of your rope. You just want to crawl into bed, pull the covers over your head, and sleep for a hundred years.

Okay, great, says God. Now we can start!

That's right. When you're weak and spent and feel you have nothing left—no energy, no resources, no pride, no nothing—then God can finally begin helping you in a *serious* way. As St. Augustine once said, when your hands are full—full of pride and strength and self-love—God can't really give you anything. But when your hands are empty and outstretched and utterly powerless—ah, then God can give you all the help you need. And your hands are free to accept it too.

"But no!" you shout. "My family is falling apart. My wife just left me. I just lost my job. I'm filing for bankruptcy. I've just been embroiled in a huge scandal, and my reputation is ruined. I'm done with false hope."

"Enough!" God says. "My grace is sufficient!"

"But I'm grieving. I just lost someone I loved very much, and I can't even get myself to breathe, much less function."

Okay, if someone close to you has died, you need to grieve. You need to grieve as long as it takes. You need to cry to the very end of your tears. And anyone who tells you differently should mind his or her own business. But eventually, when you're ready to throw off the covers and get out of bed again and venture back into the world, the same message still applies to you.

"My grace is sufficient." No more asking for signs. No more listening for special voices from Heaven. No more looking for visions. Grieve as much and as long and as hard as you like. Grieve for years if you need to. But when you're finally ready to move forward, the first thing you have to do is stop complaining about your fate.

That's not being harsh. That's being *real.* Look, even if you're not religious—even if you don't believe in God—you still have to stop complaining and take ownership at some point. We've all read stories about people who have suffered greatly and yet have somehow managed to triumph over adversity. I don't have to remind you that there are lots of people out there who are in more pain than you—people whose problems are even worse than yours. We all know that there are children starving in third-world countries. There are people with terminal diseases who are worried that their kids are going to grow up without two loving parents. There are paraplegics and quadriplegics and others who have suffered terribly debilitating accidents. All you have to do is turn on the news to see all the depressing stories about people who are suffering. And yet many of the same folks experiencing these torments are able to remain optimistic and keep their hope and faith intact. Human beings have the power to *choose* to overcome almost any kind of challenge if they really want to. "It's not your conditions but your *decisions* that determine your destiny." We've heard that line over and over from the gurus in the personal-development industry, haven't we?

But just because we've heard it so many times doesn't mean it's not true. It happens to be a fact. Where there's life, there's hope. If you're breathing right now, then it's still possible for you to turn things around. If your heart is beating, there's still time left to change.

I'm going to try to help you to do that in the following pages. But for now, only one thing is necessary. But it's *so* necessary that if you don't do it, you might as well just throw this book out. It's step one on the road to transforming your life from head to soul. And in some ways, it's the most important step because it makes all the other steps possible.

Whether you take the advice of God the Father or *The Godfather*, please, for just a little while, take a vacation from complaining. For the next few days, even if you don't feel like it, even if every atom in your body cries out against it, get off your pity-pot, put on your big-girl panties, pull yourself up by the bootstraps, and *act like a man*!

Remember: "My grace is sufficient."

Action Items

- ✓ Make a list of the five to ten things you complain about most. Then, for the remainder of this month, stop complaining about them! If you start to complain out of habit, calmly pause, re-collect yourself, and break off the complaint in mid-sentence or mid-thought. Keep doing that till you get a handle on this problem.

Be Honest about Yourself

So far, I've told you to wake up and to stop complaining—and we've barely even started. Maybe you think I'm badgering you? I'm not.

What I'm doing is taking a chance. I'm taking a chance that you're really serious about life and happiness and the need to do things differently from now on. And because I'm taking that chance, I'm going to add another little "rant" to the list: after you stop whining, the next thing you have to do is be *honest* about yourself.

So many people today kid themselves about the way they really are. They think they're doing just fine, especially when it comes to their spirituality. They're not criminals, after all—they're "good people." In the words of C. S. Lewis, they believe they've built up a healthy "credit balance" with God and that, compared with all those other sinners out there who are so obviously bad, they're doing very well.

And comparatively speaking, they might be right.

But that's not what we're talking about here. Life isn't a game of comparisons. Yes, that's the way many people treat it. But that's also why so many people are unhappy. What we're trying to aim for now is honesty—radical honesty. If you want to be happy and fulfilled and at peace, you have to forget about comparisons with other people and focus on the truth about yourself.

And what is that truth?

The truth is that you love God all right—until you stub your little toe! Then all the love goes right out the window! We talked a few pages ago about how we're all complainers. The moment we're faced with a little trial—and I'm talking about a *little* trial—we start cursing and gritting our teeth and getting frustrated completely out of proportion to the pain we're in.

We're all so attached to our favorite little comforts. Forget about the big attachments—like status and possessions and sex. I'm talking about all the tiny things you hardly ever notice, like being attached to your e-mail or your cell phone, or your Facebook or Twitter or Instagram account, or your music or a certain TV show or a certain snack. What happens when you can't indulge in one of *those* things? How irritated and frustrated do you get?

I know some spiritual people who are always trying to give things up for God. Always trying to discern what they can *do* for God. Some of them have even left their jobs and their homes and their families and traveled halfway across the world because they felt God was calling them to be missionaries—to give up their lives and sacrifice "all" for Him. And they were happy to do it.

But the truth is, one or two of these folks were happy to do it because they *wanted* to run away from life. They were tired of responsibilities. They were tired of obligations. What they really wanted was a huge change, a huge distraction. And so it was easy for them to "sacrifice" their present lives. Meanwhile, if these same people had to do something that was truly against their nature—such as cutting down on their morning coffee or exercising patience when dealing with people who irritate them—they would get all bent out of shape and have a hard time maintaining their composure.

Maybe that sounds too harsh. I don't think so. Of course some people are called to do missionary work in foreign lands. Of course that's a high and heroic calling. But those people are a minority. And that kind of decision requires a lot of discernment. Before you go trekking across the globe to do God's will in Bangladesh, you had better first make sure that what you're not *really* trying to do is run away from doing God's will right here at home.

C. S. Lewis had another good insight about this. Remember, Lewis was one of the greatest Christian writers of the twentieth century. His books are famous for their clarity, their common sense, and their persuasiveness. And Lewis lived what he wrote too. He was a genuinely good man. Yet, in one of his personal letters, he admitted to a friend that when he really, truly examined his own thinking process, he discovered that one out of every three thoughts was devoted to vanity and "self-admiration."[1] In other words, practically all he ever thought about was himself—how he looked, how he sounded, what impression he was making, how things were affecting him and his emotional state, and so forth.

After realizing how vain he really was, Lewis felt disgusted. But that isn't the point. The point is that at least he was being honest. At least he wasn't kidding himself. What about you and me? Can we do the same thing? If you analyzed all the thoughts that went through your mind during the course of an average hour, how many of them would be about you?

Not many, you say? I say, stop lying to yourself! If you want to put on a show for everyone else, that's one thing. But if you try to fool yourself, you're just a silly ass!

The late Stephen Covey talked about the three selves we all have. The first is our public self. That's the person we show the

[1] Letter to Arthur Greeves, January 30, 1930, in *The Collected Letters of C. S. Lewis*, vol. 1, *Family Letters, 1905–1931* (New York: HarperCollins, 2004), 878.

world: the person we are at work, the one we display to strangers, acquaintances, and friends. That's the self that's always on its best behavior. Then there's our private self. That's who we are at home: the person we show to our spouse and our children.

You don't have to be a psychologist to know there's often a huge difference between these two parts of our character. We all know people who are friendly and charming and funny to everyone they know, but the second they get home and let their hair down, they start yelling at the people they supposedly love the most. That's pretty common, wouldn't you say?

But there's another self too, a third part of our character that neither the world nor our families see. And that's our inner, secret self.

The secret self is that part of our identity we keep most private. We don't show it to anyone. We don't even like to show it to ourselves. When C. S. Lewis admitted that a third of his thoughts focused on vanity, this is what he was exposing. It's what we're truly thinking and feeling in that inner stream of consciousness, from moment to moment. And the reason most of us would never reveal it—even to our closest friends—is that it's simply too embarrassing.

You know what I'm talking about! It's our secret self that feels all the pride and anger and jealousy and greed and resentment and laziness and envy and lust. It's our secret self that's constantly monitoring and calculating what other people think of us—i.e., how much they admire us—based on what we say and do. It's our secret self that feels that little twinge of pleasure when things go wrong for other people. It's the part of us that's always looking for sex or power or status, no matter how much we may be smiling and what pleasant nonsense comes out of our mouths. And sometimes—hopefully not too often—these hidden desires of ours are so twisted and so devious and so perverted and so *wrong* that we can't even bring ourselves to admit that they're real, that they're actually part of our makeup.

And yet they are.

Now, the personal-development people tell us that, to a large extent, our happiness as human beings depends on how *congruent* we are—how much *in sync* these three aspects of our character are with one another. If your public self is radically different from your private self, you're going to have problems. If your secret self is radically different from your private self, you're going to have problems.

And doesn't that make sense? If you live a life of hypocrisy, you're never going to be at peace. For centuries, the greatest philosophers and theologians have taught that happiness is tied to the principles of harmony and balance. Well, how in the world can you lead a harmonious, balanced life if all three of your selves are so out of line, or—even worse—if they're warring with one another? We see this sometimes with political and religious leaders who are ruined by public scandals. When these figures fall from grace, isn't it always because they were leading double lives, lives that were radically opposed to each other?

Yes, it's possible through duplicity and lying to live in a kind of fractured state for a long time without getting caught. Some people are very skilled at it. But it's just plain impossible to be happy while doing it.

And to make matters even more complicated, there's an additional challenge—one that the personal-development people don't usually tell you about. There are some people who can appear to have perfectly balanced and harmonious personalities and *still* be miserable. That's right. There doesn't have to be any conflict within them, and they can still have wretched lives. The reason is that they can be mean—publicly, privately, *and* secretly. They can be nasty all the way through, and the result will still be that they're unhappy, frustrated human beings.

There are people like that out there, aren't there? People like Dickens's famous character Ebenezer Scrooge. I'm sure you know some. The point is that harmony and balance and congruency aren't the only ingredients necessary for happiness. There's something else too. And that something has to do with God and *His* vision for you, with the person that *He* created you to be, with the self that *He* sees: with your *divine* self.

We'll have a lot more to say about this later on, but for now, the only thing that matters is that we're honest. The world is always saying that we're okay, that we're doing fine, that if only we loved ourselves "just the way we are," everything would be wonderful. The dirtiest word in the English language today is *guilt*. According to the world, all of us have way too much guilt—most of it caused by our backward Christian upbringing. Anytime we feel guilt of any kind, our society tells us that it's unhealthy and that we need to get rid of it as fast as we can. That's what all the talk shows and media advise, isn't it? They're always glossing over the fact that human beings really do act badly, that we really do think badly, and that there really are terrible things about us that need to change.

But we're not going to gloss over anything here. We're not going to pull punches or make any rationalizations. If you get one thing out of this book, let it be that you stop kidding yourself. You know what goes on in your brain. You know what you're thinking from moment to moment. And, my friend, you know that a lot of it is just garbage.

The same thing goes for me. The same thing goes for your parents. The same thing goes for your children. The same thing goes for the pastor at your church. The same thing goes for the president. The same thing goes for the pope! We all know the truth about one another. We're *all* sinners. The good news is that once we recognize the ugliness and admit it to ourselves in complete, radical honesty, at least we can move forward.

And that's exactly what we're going to do.

Action Items

- ✓ Write four paragraphs to describe each of your four "selves." Describe your public self, your private self, and your secret self (if you need to use abbreviations or code words for your most embarrassing faults and sins, go ahead). Finally, take a shot at describing your divine self. What is the kind of person you think God wants you to be? Feel free to make these descriptions as long or short as you like—but be honest!

You Are One Person: Body, Mind, and Spirit

There are four basic, foundational principles that all of us have to get into our heads—not only now but for the rest of our lives.

Long after you finish this book and forget most of what's in it, you're going to continue to experience all the joys and agonies that go along with living in this world. But there are four "starting points" you have to keep coming back to, no matter what happens and no matter how bad or good things are; four pillars on which the foundation of a consistently happy life needs to be built.

The first of these pillars has to do with the body-mind-spirit connection, and it's what I'd like to concentrate on today.

When things are going wrong and you're not happy and not at peace, you can't just think that you're going to change one thing and your whole life will be miraculously transformed. It won't, because "what's wrong" with your life is almost never just one thing. It's everything. It's the whole thing. It's all connected.

When you try to separate the body, the mind, and the spirit and excel in one particular area, you might very well have some degree of success, but your life, as a whole, is not going to benefit—in fact, your life, as a whole, might even suffer.

Think of it this way: If you move your left leg in one direction, and your right leg in the other, you're not going to go anywhere, are you? You're going to be stuck in the same position. Or if you're driving your car and you try to step on the gas with one foot and the brake with the other, you're going to come to a screeching halt, right? And you'll probably do some damage to your vehicle, too.

The same concept applies here.

You're a human being. That means you're a *combination* of body, mind, and spirit. You're not just one entity. You're not pure spirit or mind, like the angels, and you're not pure matter, like the book or tablet you're holding in your hand. You're all three, at the very same time. That's the thing that separates you from the rest of creation. And all three—body, mind, and spirit—are "wired" together, intricately and seamlessly.

What's the practical result? Well, it means that if you stuff yourself with food and continually overeat, you might not just gain weight—you might also start feeling lazy or spiritually dry or sexually tempted, or you might find that it's easier for you to lie or cheat or lose your temper. The reason is that your body is wired to your spirit.

And if you read a thousand books in an effort to improve your mind but fail to exercise spiritual charity and humility, you may end up knowing a lot of useless facts and acquire the reputation of a scholar, but underneath you might still be a hypocrite who's wrong on the most basic moral and ethical issues. Do you know any people like that? Any college professors, maybe? Any elected officials? I do! The reason is that the mind and the spirit are wired together and can't be separated. If you do something bad to one, the other is going to be affected in some way.

Now, *how* everything is connected is a little difficult to understand—even for the greatest theologians—and could easily be the subject of a whole book. But the bottom line is that it has to do with your *will*. Remember, all the decisions you make in life are controlled by your God-given free will. Try to picture this diagram. On one side you have all your *desires*—the desires of your body, the desires of your mind, and the desires of your spirit. And on the other side you have your *conscience*—the knowledge of right and wrong, the knowledge of which desires you should say yes to and which you should say no to. Over and above both of these is your will, which acts as the arbiter and judge between the two.

Your will is constantly making decisions. Day in, day out, year in, year out, in thousands of different situations, your will is *choosing*. And the more you give in to desires that are not good for you—that is, the more you disobey your conscience—the more your will is weakened. The will is just like a muscle. It needs to be exercised in order to stay strong. When you don't exercise it, it shrivels up and loses all its strength. Then, when it's called upon to make tough decisions in other areas of your life, it's not able to.

That's why people are always complaining that they have no willpower. They've lost it because they've made hundreds and hundreds of bad choices that have essentially caused their will to atrophy, thereby losing its ability to choose wisely or to stick to choices it knows are correct.

It's so important for you to get what I'm saying here. Everything is intertwined! It's all part of the same system. When you give in to one particular desire that's wrong—be it physical, intellectual, or spiritual—you weaken the whole system and make it easier to succumb to other desires that aren't good for you. And those other desires might be totally different from the ones you originally made bad choices about. When you weaken the will, you lose power everywhere in life. You darken your intellect so it can't see what's right. You disable your body so it can't fight temptation. You deaden your spirit so it can't resist sin. You de-energize everything.

You're really a very incredible creation—a well-balanced, harmonious, integrated machine—and if you screw around with one part of it, you're going to cause the whole thing to break down.

What this means, practically, is that you have no choice but to take a holistic, "total person" approach to life, especially when it comes to seeking happiness. You can't simply lose weight and expect to be happy. You can't simply make more money and expect to be happy. You can't simply read a bunch of books—or write them, for that matter—and expect to be happy. You can't even just pray and expect to be happy. Even the holiest hermits have to get out into the open air and exercise once in a while in order to clear their heads. Otherwise, their interior prayer life would eventually dry up. It has to—it's a law of the universe, a law put there by God Himself when He created us.

Look, you *know* this is true—especially in the area of morality. You know that you can't practice vice virtuously. Let me repeat that: *You can't practice vice virtuously.*

A person who embezzles from his job is going to be the same kind of person who cheats on his taxes, the same kind of person who is dishonest about money in general. A person who is slovenly and sloppy and disorganized in his professional life is also going to be slovenly, sloppy, and disorganized in the way he thinks—and probably in his relationships as well. A person who is addicted to pornography is going to be the same kind of person who lies to his spouse and has affairs with other women (if given the right opportunity). He's not going to be a loving, honest, adoring, faithful husband. And if you think otherwise, you're living in a fantasy world.

Oh, sure, you may be able to get away with "compartmentalizing" your ethics for a while—cheating in one area and trying to be "pure" in another—but it won't work for long, and certainly not forever. The same goes for the other parts of your life that aren't directly connected to morality. Plenty of people have satisfactory work lives but miserable marriages. Or wonderfully fit bodies but emotional lives that are a wreck. Or stimulating intellectual lives but terribly unhealthy eating habits. People function all the time in this fractured, compartmentalized way. But it can't work forever. Eventually your life is going to fall apart. It has to—because the foundation of the entire structure, your will, is the thing that has been eroded.

That's one of the main themes of the book *Dr. Jekyll and Mr. Hyde*: you can't cut yourself off from your conscience; the amputation is always a failure. Listen, if you chop a worm into sections, the severed pieces can still live and move. But you're not a worm! You're a human being, made in the image and likeness of God. You have a certain physical, psychological, and spiritual unity. You can't be sliced apart into separate living entities, like some grotesque slithering invertebrate.

And even if you could live that way, I'm certainly not going to help you do it. This book is not about functioning or coping. It's about happiness. And to be truly happy, truly fulfilled, and truly at peace, you have to be improving in every area of your life at the same time. You have to commit to working on the big picture—on the whole enchilada!

So for the last time, understand that you are *one* person—body, mind, and spirit. That's the way you need to view yourself for the rest of your life.

Make sense? Then let's move on to the second lifetime principle.

Action Items

- ✓ Think about your own mind-body-spirit connection. Is there anything counterproductive you are doing in one area that might be adversely affecting another area? This is a difficult question so think hard! Then write down the answer.
- ✓ Next write down three things you can do to improve your health or level of physical fitness, three things you can do to improve your mind, and three things you can do to nourish your spirituality and your relationship with God. These things don't have to be big—in fact, they should be reasonably simple and easy to accomplish. Moreover, you don't have to do these things yet. What's important is that you write them down clearly and succinctly. We'll be referring back to this list later.

About-Face!

How many times have you wanted to start fresh? How many times have you said to yourself, "If only I could begin from square one, everything would be different"?

But you can't ever seem to get back to square one, can you?

Well, guess what? You never will.

People complain all the time that they could solve their financial problems if only they had no preexisting debt. Or they could solve their relationship problems if only they didn't have so much pent-up animosity from past fights. Or they could solve their overeating problems if only they could instantaneously lose the fifty extra pounds they put on because of stress. Or they could solve their spiritual problems if only they could forget the guilt heaped on them by the Church when they were younger.

Excuses, excuses! Nothing but excuses!

The point is not to try to erase your past and start at square one. You left square one in the dust a long time ago. The point is not to begin at the beginning. That's gone. History. You're never going to see it again. The point is to turn around and *start over.*

What are the first commands they teach you in the military? In basic training, they show you a lot of things: how to keep physically fit; how to clean, assemble, and use your rifle; how to march; how to drill—and how to "about-face."

"About-face" simply means to turn around and go in the opposite direction. The sergeants yelling at you during boot camp don't tell you to go back to the starting point. They don't tell you to find the spot on the field where you were standing when the march began. They don't care where the heck you came from or where the heck you happen to be. All they care about is that you stop in your tracks and go the other way.

In war—and make no mistake, life can sometimes be a war—when you discover that you're marching into enemy territory, you have to be ready to reverse yourself. There's no time for soul-searching. No time for self-pity. No time for self-recrimination. No time for worrying about where you began or how you got there. There's no time for anything. You just have to turn your butt around and get going!

And that's lifetime principle number two. If you see that you're headed in the wrong direction, the first thing you have to do is stop everything—including your self-loathing and your self-analysis and whatever else you're brooding about—and make a decision to reverse the behavior that's causing you to go down that road.

Too simple, you say?

Baloney! It's not. It's the only thing you *can* do. It's the only choice you have. I'm not saying it's easy. Sometimes it's the most difficult thing in the world. I'm just saying it's simple. It's foundational. It's the only sensible course open to you.

You have to be really honest with yourself now. Is what you're doing today moving you closer to where you want to be tomorrow? If not, you have to stop and about-face. I'm sure you know this already. You might even know exactly what you have to do—or at least you have a general idea. But the old cliché is true: it's not a case of knowing what to do; it's a case of *doing what you know*.

So many people don't believe they have the power to turn around. They've been through life's ups and downs so many times that they've lost all confidence in themselves. But that's nonsense. As all the personal-development people will tell you, your past is not your future!

Do you hear? Your past is not your future!

Yes, that might be another cliché. So what? So your past is full of garbage. So you've screwed up a million times. So you're "damaged goods." We all are. It's impossible not to be damaged in this world. Practically everything the world tells us about values and happiness and pleasure is wrong, so of course we're going to be screwed up. And more significantly, the people around us are going to be screwed up too, and they're going to hurt us as a result. It's a vicious circle. Get used to it.

Believe me, I'm not trying to give anyone a free pass. I'm only saying that if the morality of the world is going to pot, it's naïve to think that you and I aren't going to be affected in a very personal way. We're going to have lots of temptations and lots of wounds and scars. It's just a fact. As one Southern preacher put it, "If you soak in a tub of manure long enough, you just might end up smelling funny." And that's the state of society today. Some of us smell pretty funny.

So what can you do about it? There's only one sane option: to move forward in the right direction. The problem is that you can't move forward if you keep fixating on what happened to you in the past. There's a great saying about this too: "You'll never be able to drive anywhere if all you ever do is look in the rearview mirror." That's exactly how many of us live our lives. We spend all our time looking in the rearview mirror instead of keeping our eyes on the road ahead of us.

Now, maybe you think *I'm* being the naïve one. Maybe you think I'm underestimating the weight of the emotional baggage everyone is carrying around. I'm not. Listen, I've got plenty of my own emotional baggage. I've messed up quite a bit in my life. I've done things I'm ashamed of, I've failed in relationships, I've failed in businesses, I've acted stupidly and selfishly, I've hurt people I loved, and I've had my own heart broken into little pieces on more than one occasion. As Frank Sinatra sings in the song "That's Life," I've been "up and down and over and out"—lots of times!

So trust me, I'm not claiming you can make the past magically disappear and reinvent yourself in the blink of an eye. It's going to take a lot of hard work, and it's going to involve looking at the world in an entirely different way. That's one of the purposes of this book—to help you do that. But the point is that you can't even start until you make a decision to turn around. And that's what we're talking about now. The *decision*.

My goodness, I know some people who have pasts that would make you want to cry. People whose children died in horrible fires; people who were physically abused by family members for years; people who were sexually molested in the most cruel and unspeakable ways; people who have lost everything because of their addiction to drugs and alcohol and pornography. I know one woman who had sixteen abortions! You heard me—*sixteen*!

Of course, it's going to take time and serious counseling to heal those kinds of lacerating wounds. One of the reasons the personal-development industry falls so short of the mark so often is that it's afraid to talk about the only kind of healing that really works over the long term, the only kind that really sticks—the healing that comes from God.

The Bible makes some pretty mind-blowing promises. It claims, for instance, that the kind of peace you can have if you follow God's will is so special and so complete and so unlike anything else you've ever experienced, it "transcends all understanding"

(Phil. 4:7, NIV). The Bible also says, in one famous passage from the book of Revelation, that God will "make all things new" (Rev. 21:5). *New.*

This is deep stuff. It's not something you hear from armchair therapists or TV talk-show hosts or self-help experts. God doesn't ever say He's going to take you back to square one or let you start at the beginning. He doesn't even promise that He'll give you any big psychological breakthroughs in terms of understanding your past. In fact, you can search all of Scripture, and you won't find a single verse that says, "Blessed are they who understand." Instead, what you'll find is "Take up your cross and follow me" (see Matt. 16:24).

If you do *that*—take up your cross and follow God—then God pledges that He'll make everything in your life brand-new. He'll take all that has ever happened to you in the past—all the screw-ups and all the suffering and all the evil—and *transform* it into something else, something unexpected, something that actually gives you strength and peace and happiness. That's what authentic Christian spirituality has to offer.

But for those kinds of profound, transformative experiences to take place, certain other decisions have to be made first—decisions involving faith and repentance and forgiveness. We'll be talking about each of those in its proper place. But we're not quite ready for them yet. The only decision we're concerned with here is the one to turn around. And that decision can be made at any time, even if you don't yet believe in God or Christianity or Catholicism or the spiritual world. It's a decision that takes just a second to make. But oh, what an important second! It's a second that can literally mean the difference between life and death.

The best thing is that there's time to do it right now. After all, you haven't fallen off any cliff yet, have you? Not if you're breathing. Not if you're reading these words. Where there's life, there's hope. Don't ever forget that! So even if you've "turned around" hundreds of times before, you still have to muster the courage to say: "Enough! I've had it! I'm going to do an about-face, and I'm going to do things right for a change."

I promise that if you sincerely try to implement what you read in these pages, this time *will* be different for you.

Action Items

- ✓ Pick one thing you've been doing wrong and stop doing it *now*. It doesn't have to be something very difficult to stop (like an addiction to smoking). It can be something easier. Write it down in your notebook and do an immediate about-face. If you want to stop doing several things that's okay, but pick at least one.

Momentum Is the Key

In order to properly understand the third lifetime principle, we're going to have to do some physics. Remember physics from school? Remember all the laws of the universe? The law of gravity? The laws of conservation of matter and energy?

Well, there was another law they taught us that's absolutely essential if we want to understand why life can be so unhappy and why it can be so difficult to change. It's called the *law of inertia.*

Do you recall what this law states? "An object at rest tends to stay at rest."

If a car is parked on the street with the engine turned off, it's not going to move anywhere—at least not on its own. It's going to stay right there. If a chair is placed next to a desk and no one touches it, it's going to remain in that position gathering dust till kingdom come. Things don't move by themselves; something must *make* them move. That couldn't be simpler, right?

But guess what? The law of inertia is true not only in physics; it's true in every area of life. It's true for human beings. It's true for businesses. It's true for governments. It's especially true for people who are experiencing different kinds of funks. When you're overweight and out of shape, you're essentially "at rest," and you tend to "stay at rest." You don't want to go to the gym and exercise, or lift weights, or run, or eat healthy foods. When you're disorganized and sloppy and your life is a big mess, you're "at rest" and tend to "stay at rest." You don't want to straighten everything up or do a major house cleaning or even dress nicely. When your finances are in shambles and you owe everybody money, you're "at rest" and tend to "stay at rest." You don't want to make the hard choices necessary to correct the situation. You don't want to cut your expenses drastically or stop using your credit cards. You don't want to even look at your bills. Instead, you want to watch TV, or have a drink, or eat, or gamble, or play video games, or go on vacation, or have sex. Anything to distract you from your problems.

Why? Because nobody wants pain! Looking at a balance sheet when we know our finances are a wreck is painful. Looking in the mirror when we're disgusted with all our flab is painful. The only time we get off our butts and take action is when the pain of *not* doing something becomes so great that it exceeds the pain of doing it. In other words, we sometimes get *so* upset by the way things are that we push ourselves *through* the pain and *move*.

One of the personal-development experts—I think it was Tony Robbins—called this phenomenon the "pressure cooker." We indulge in behavior that isn't good for us, and as a result, bad things start to happen. This causes us to feel pain, and we have the desire to change—but the effort required is too difficult, so we don't try. Instead, the pressure builds and builds until it gets so great that we *have to* do something—otherwise there will be an explosion. But then, once we finally take action and things start to improve, the pressure lets off for a while—and guess what happens? We start the same old bad behavior again. Almost immediately, the pressure begins to build. And so we go through the process over and over again.

Is that your life? A pressure cooker? Is that the way you want to spend the tiny amount of time you have on this planet?

Listen, there's a better way to get yourself to move, a better way to overcome the law of inertia—one that doesn't require explosive pressure. It involves another principle from physics. It's called *momentum*.

Follow me here! This is one of the most important things in life to learn. And it's so simple that people forget it all the time. When an object at rest starts to move, it moves slowly at first. It doesn't go at full speed instantaneously. It accelerates. It *builds* momentum. I've done a lot of traveling on planes in my life. In fact, I happen to be a pilot. When you're on the runway and you begin your takeoff roll, you don't just miraculously lift off the ground. You wait for the tower to say, "Clear for takeoff." Then you push the throttle forward, and the plane begins to inch along. At first, you're going very slowly—so slowly that a child could easily outrun you. Then, as the seconds tick by, your speed picks up, and before you know it, you're airborne.

This is true for everything in life.

The key to taking effective, long-lasting action is momentum. If you want to get out of a funk—any funk—the best thing to do is to start with small actions, even the tiniest ones, but to take them consistently over the period of a few days and weeks. Once you do that, things are bound to accelerate.

You *know* this works. You've been through it before. You know that first trip to the gym is the hardest. It's actually torture to force yourself to go. The second trip is a little easier. The third easier still. By the fourth time, you're raring to go. In fact, nothing can stop you from going. The same applies to getting yourself organized. Or straightening out your finances. Or even fixing your relationships. If you start small and force yourself through the initial period of pain, you *will* pick up speed. It's just a law of the universe.

And even if it takes longer than you expect to build momentum, small steps are still the key to success. I don't care how cliché this sounds, but slow and steady always wins the race. Always.

Ernest Hemingway was one of the most important writers who ever lived. His novels and short stories changed literature forever. But do you know how much he wrote a day? A mere 250 words! Once in a while, he got lucky and was able to write 500. But that was rare. In all his years of writing, he never cared about putting thousands of words down on paper, as so many other authors do. He just wanted to write "a good 250." But he wanted to do it consistently. He knew that if he did that every day, he would have a whole book by the end of the year.

Do you realize that? Do you realize that if you wrote a steady 250 words a day, you could have a novel done within twelve months?

We've all got to get off this roller coaster we're on. Up and down, up and down. It never stops. How many "phases" have you gone through in your life? We're always going through "phases." Isn't it pathetic? We're always getting excited about this thing or that. Always trying some fad diet or exercise plan or personal-development program. They all work for a while but then lose their power once the emotional high is gone. We're like dumb mice that keep going for the same piece of cheese in the same mousetrap, no matter how many times we get caught. Aren't you tired of it?

But if you start small and build slowly—or even if you just keep up the same pace—your progress won't stop with such depressing regularity. Life won't be a roller coaster or a pressure cooker or a series of phases anymore.

Wouldn't that be nice?

This isn't just some personal-development principle. It's at the heart of true spirituality. The Bible warns us not to despise small beginnings or small things. And if you look through Scripture, you'll find dozens of examples of battles in which a handful of warriors was able to miraculously defeat a huge army. God always seems to go out of His way to show that small numbers of people—or even people of small stature—have the power to overcome overwhelming odds, as long as He is on their side.

The best example of this, of course, is the story of how God saved humanity. Now, nothing is bigger or greater or more powerful than God, right? And yet, when this same Almighty God chose to enter human history and become a man, He did so by first becoming a little baby. We can't ever forget that Jesus Christ—who Christians believe *is* God—was born a child and placed in a small manger. And before that, He was an embryo in His Mother's womb. And before that, He was a zygote—just two cells, yet divine! Consider the implications! If God Himself thought it was best to start small, why wouldn't we use the same strategy?

Building momentum always works. It doesn't matter if you're eighteen or eighty, broke or a billionaire, the worst sinner in the world or the greatest saint. Sometimes the results aren't always immediate, but that's to be expected. You don't plant seeds at night and expect flowers to be blooming the next morning, do you? It takes time before you can reap what you sow. But you've got to start sowing. You've got to get the seeds in the ground!

If you're in lousy physical shape and need to start an exercise routine, of course it would be great if you could begin going to the gym regularly. But if you can't bring yourself to do that right now, fine. Take a walk around the block instead. Or drink a few extra glasses of water. Or buy an exercise book and read the first chapter. It's not really important what you do as long as you do *something*—and as long as you *keep* doing a little something extra every day.

Or if your life is a chaotic mess, then start organizing a *tiny* part of it. Go clean your closet! Who cares if some people think that's silly? Who cares if it's a cliché? Who cares if you've got much bigger concerns? The point is that it works. It gets the juices flowing. It gives you the feeling that you're in control of your life—and that's something that's absolutely necessary if you're ever going to solve all your other problems.

Remember, this is just a starting point. But it's a starting point you've got to keep coming back to. Gravity is always going to be pulling you down. Stumbling blocks are always going to be thrust in your way. And when you run across them and they halt your progress, you've got to be able to jump-start yourself with a minimum amount of turmoil. No more pressure cooker! Whether it's your body, your mind, or your spirit we're working on, it's always best to take baby steps first.

Of course, you have to get radical too. It's impossible to be happy if you're not radical in your approach to life and in your approach to God. We said in the very first chapter that you can have great health, great relationships, and a billion dollars and still be a slave to your attachments and a miserable wretch. We're going to address all that, don't worry. But at this stage it's better to just concentrate on *moving*.

So don't despise small beginnings! Pick a few random things right now—a few nagging tasks, a few irritating to-do items you haven't been able to get done in the last few months—and start working on them, slowly. Resist the urge to do it all at once. Consistency is what we're aiming for. Momentum is what we're aiming for.

Go do something small!

Action Items

- ✓ In deciding which two or three small things to do, go back to the list you made at the end of Day 4 and review it carefully.

Rest, Review, Celebrate

Congratulations! You made it through Week 1.

Today is a day of rest. Rest is sacred. Rest is holy. Rest is necessary. We know that when God created the heavens and the earth, He rested on the seventh day. You should too! Today is a day to review your notes from the past six days and celebrate your accomplishments. If you started this program on a Monday, today is also a day to go to church and give thanks to God for guiding you down this wonderful path of transformation and self-renewal. If you don't believe in God or if you have issues with organized religion or the Church, there's no need for alarm. We'll be talking more about these important topics soon. For now, try to at least keep an open mind. Be confident that you're doing a great job and that even better things are in store for you. In the meantime, reward yourself by doing something fun.

See you tomorrow!

Take Control

Personal Development Is Not Enough

The fourth basic lifetime principle we're going to discuss has to do with the G-word. "God."

Now, I've mentioned God and Christianity and Catholicism and the Bible in this book but not that much. I certainly haven't beaten you over the head with religion, have I?

The reason is *not* that it's not important. It's that it's *so* important I didn't want you to just dismiss what I was saying because you happen to be an atheist or an agnostic or because you're angry at God or the Church or at "organized religion" in general.

Nowadays people hear you say the word "God," and they get so nervous. They automatically think you're going to start preaching to them. Well, I'm not a preacher. But I *am* going to give you a little sermon right now on the truth about life. In fact, it may be the most important sermon you'll ever hear. And I don't intend to dilute it or sugarcoat it in any way. I'm just going to give it to you straight.

If you think you're going to make it through this crazy, schizophrenic world of ours, with all its ups and downs and pains and pleasures, and somehow manage to experience peace and happiness without paying any attention to what God wants from you, you're really kidding yourself. I don't care how successful you are or how many personal-development courses you've taken or how much you think you've got it all together; the moment life really slams you in the face with a two-by-four (and if it hasn't already, trust me, it will) your whole pretty, phony, fragile façade of contentment is going to come crumbling down.

And not only that, but even if nothing bad ever happens to you, you *still* wouldn't get anywhere near true peace and happiness. Notice I didn't say you couldn't make lots of money and have lots of pleasures and lots of sexy distractions. Nor did I say that you couldn't have lots of wonderful, loving experiences with your family and friends. I said you couldn't get to true peace and happiness. Unless you understand what those terms really mean, and unless you understand how following God's plan will get you there, you're never going to understand why so many people fail in their quest to attain them.

Think about a map for a minute. Stephen Covey, who wrote the bestselling book *The 7 Habits of Highly Effective People*, made a great point about maps. He said that if you wanted to get to a certain place in New York City but had never been there before, you might go out and buy one of those cheap maps they sell on the street. But what if there had been an error in the printing of the map? What if the mapmaker had accidentally labeled the map "New York City" when it was really a map of Chicago?

If you tried to follow that map, it would be pretty confusing, wouldn't it? You'd try to go down the right streets and make the correct turns, but you'd keep ending up at the wrong place. You'd go in a bunch of different directions, but you'd still be lost. And yet, if you looked down at the map, it would say very clearly "New York City."

That's exactly what our society has done to people today. It has given us a map that's labeled "Happiness" and urged us to follow it. Only it's not a map to Happiness at all. It's a map to "Success" or to "Self-Improvement" or to "Worldly Pleasures" or to "Sex without Responsibility" or to "Style and Cool" or to who knows what. Most times, it ends up being a map to Misery. But the wrong label has been stuck on it, and it's been sold to us anyway. And like sheep, we blindly follow it and then scratch our heads and wonder why we never arrive at our destination.

Well, there *is* an accurate map that exists. And it's the map that has been provided to us by God Himself in the form of His Ten Commandments, His laws, His Word, and primarily the Church He founded. This map has one main destination: Heaven. And surprisingly, God has made the gigantic claim that if you follow this map and attempt to reach that destination, you'll actually experience peace and happiness *along the way*. Therefore, it's a map that gives you two destinations for the price of one: Heaven in the world to come, and peace and happiness right now.

We're going to be talking more about this map later, but for now, understand that a lot of people don't like it. Some don't believe it to begin with. Others find it too difficult to follow. After all, it doesn't exactly provide us with the easiest route of passage. In fact, it takes us through some pretty rough terrain. Some of the roads are rocky and winding and pretty scary. And it often leads us through climates that are dark and stormy. The map promises peace and happiness, but paradoxically, it also promises that we have to suffer and, in the process, might even be persecuted. People don't want to hear that, do they?

But at least it's a map that claims to be true, and at least it's one that's accurately labeled. We may not always like what it says, but it's not false advertising. Not according to the Mapmaker, anyway.

The same can't be said for all the empty promises the culture tries to ram down our throats about sex and money and power and status. Even the personal-development industry—which I genuinely respect because it tries to help people—is guilty of the same defective labeling. It says it wants to assist us to make improvements in our lives, but then it leaves out the most important factor in determining what true "improvement" really depends on: following God's map.

Self-help experts claim that they can teach us to control the way we think and focus on the "positive," thereby making us more efficient, effective, and optimistic. They say that the way we think about things determines our emotional state and that, therefore, even the worst experiences can yield the best results, if we view them as "opportunities for growth."

Wonderful! All of those famous personal-development books—*As a Man Thinketh, How to Win Friends and Influence People, Think and Grow Rich,* and so on—are terrific. God bless them, every one.

But they all have the same weakness, the same Achilles' heel. They all fail to take into account the presence of God and *His* plan for us. Because of that, none of the authors of those books has the slightest clue how to teach us to live truly good, holy lives—the kind God wants us to live.

Let's use an extreme example. If Adolf Hitler had somehow been able to take a personal-development course before World War II, he wouldn't have done one thing differently to change his character or his monstrous morality—he would just have become a happier, more efficient Adolf Hitler. Let me repeat that. If self-help books and audio programs and seminars were available back in the 1930s and '40s, and Adolf Hitler made full use of them, he would simply have become a better version of his evil self!

Now, please don't misunderstand me. I'm not comparing personal-development experts to the Nazis. Nor am I saying that if you follow a self-improvement program, it's going to make you evil. It's not. I've used self-help books and audios for years and benefited greatly from them. But what I'm saying now is that they're not enough. They're deficient. In the hands of someone who's selfish or cruel or evil, they can actually do more damage than good.

The biggest problem with much of the personal-development industry is that it's *devoid* of any real moral compass. Many of today's self-help gurus are so worried that they're going to come off as too religious that they espouse the most tepid spirituality possible—and sometimes none at all. If they do bother to talk about the need to have a "relationship" with God, they conveniently lump it together with all the other areas of life that need to be improved—such as a person's finances or job or level of physical fitness.

But they've got everything backward. Of course it's important to take a holistic approach to life. As we said earlier, your body, your mind, and your spirit are all connected. But that's not the same thing as putting God on the same level as your gym membership. You can't work on spirituality the way you work on your biceps or your abs or your lower back. Your relationship with God has to inform and infuse everything you do—it has to be *over and above* everything you do.

You see, there really *is* a God, and He really *does* have a plan for us. There really are such things as good and evil, right and wrong, and objective truth. There really is a correct map to follow. And if you trivialize these things—as the personal-development industry often does—there's no chance you're ever going to experience true peace and happiness.

Well, we're not going to make the same mistake here. No matter what topics we discuss in this book, we're never going to forget the most important foundational principle of them all—we're never going to forget the answer to these three simple questions:

- Where did we come from? God.
- Where are we going? God.
- What is life about? God.

Get that right, and everything else will be a whole lot easier—okay?

End of sermon!

Action Items

- ✓ Write a paragraph about your relationship with God. Do you believe in Him? If so, are you close to Him? Would you say that your faith in Him is strong or weak or somewhere in the middle? Have you ever been angry at Him? How often do you think about Him? How often do you pray? Are you a Christian? A Catholic? If so, what is your relationship with the Church? If you don't believe in God, do you have any spiritual beliefs whatsoever? If so, what are they? Are you at least open to taking another look at the personal God of Christianity?

Spirituality 101

Let's take a few seconds to recap.

I've said some pretty tough things so far. I've said that most people are walking around like zombies, unaware that their priorities are completely screwed up. I've said that we need to stop whining and moaning and take ownership of our lives—especially when things aren't going right. I've said that most of us are kidding ourselves about who we really are; that we like to think we're such wonderful people when, in fact, our true, inner selves are a lot uglier than we would ever admit. I've tried hard not to pull any punches here. I've taken a real risk that all these "negative" statements might turn you off. But I've been willing to do that because I think it's a lot more important for you to wake up than it is for you to like me.

The good news is that no matter how bad things are, there's always time to reverse course. And so I've also gone over a few basic principles that are necessary to make any kind of progress in life. I've talked about taking a mind-body-spirit approach to everything we do; I've talked about the importance of being able to about-face whenever we realize we're headed the wrong way. I've talked about the benefit of starting with small actions in order to build momentum. And finally, I've talked about the absolute necessity of putting God first—of using *His* plan and *His* map in order to be happy—not just our own self-improvement goals.

But now it's time to get into the nitty-gritty. Now it's time to take some serious action. Over the next few days, I'm going to give you some very specific things I'd like you to try. Small things. Simple things. Not easy things—but things that are simple to understand and to implement. And right off the bat, I want to avoid that huge error the personal-development industry always seems to make—that huge error of *omission* we talked about earlier. I want to start by enlisting the help of God.

To me, what we're going to talk about now represents the basics of authentic spirituality. And I mean the *basics*.

I know that you might already be well advanced in the spiritual life. That's great. Maybe you'll want to skip over this part. But I wouldn't if I were you. The reason is that we're trying to do something different here. We're not only concentrating on the fundamentals—we're concentrating on doing the fundamentals *consistently* over your whole lifetime, so that your spirituality never deteriorates into a mere phase. You don't want to be one of those spiritual bingers, do you? You know the type—the ones who get obsessed about God and religion and then lose all their fervor after a while and stop completely. The aim of this book is not to form future lapsed Catholics. It's to help you do the right thing, *all the time*.

So, to start at the beginning . . .

When you get up in the morning, do you know the first thing you should do? I'm talking about before you even open your eyes. I'm talking about when you're still lying there in a fog, upset that you have to get out of bed and go to work. At that very moment, just as you're starting to re-enter the world of the living, you need to do one ultra-important thing. You need to say a short prayer.

Why? Because the first really conscious moment of your day should be given to God.

Now, everyone knows that prayer is the foundation of the spiritual life. There have been thousands of books written on the subject and millions of sermons preached on it. And as you get further along in the spiritual life, you'll find that there are many ways of praying. But for our purposes, there's really no need to take something so simple and make it seem complicated. Prayer is nothing more than talking to God. It's the act of communicating with our Creator and Redeemer. Period.

In order to have a relationship with God—or with anyone, for that matter—you have to communicate, right? Communication is the key. Well, prayer opens up the communication channel with God. And it doesn't take long to do. In fact, it can almost be instantaneous. After all, how long does it take you to plug in your phone or your computer or your battery charger? It's the same for your morning prayer. What you need to do when you wake up is essentially "plug yourself in" to the power source of the entire universe, the power source that created the world, that created *you*. And the way you do that is by sending up a short message to Him.

What do you say in the message? How about this: *Thank You, God, for giving me another morning. Please help me to do Your will today.*

That's it! And if you really want to cover all the bases, you can say the Our Father too. The Our Father—or the Lord's Prayer—is the prayer that Jesus Christ Himself taught. It's the prayer on which all other authentic Christian prayers are based. It contains absolutely everything you need to say to God—it praises Him, thanks Him, asks Him for help, and asks Him for forgiveness for anything you may have done wrong. Libraries of books have been written about this prayer, and whole catechisms have been organized around it. It's the model for all genuine prayer.

And it's so short. Do you know how long it takes to say good morning to God and then add an Our Father? Twenty-two seconds. That's right. I just timed it. And I said it very slowly too. Can you spare twenty-two seconds every morning for the rest of your life, for the One who gave you life?

You don't think you can? You don't know if you have enough faith yet?

Listen. If you truly feel you can't say this little prayer because you don't believe in God, then all you have to do is incorporate that doubt into the prayer itself. In other words, you can bring your lack of faith right to God's doorstep. You can say: *God, I really don't know if I believe in You yet. But if You're there, thanks for giving me another morning. And by the way, can You please increase my faith?*

Now, that's as honest and sincere as you can get. There's nothing wrong with a prayer like that. It even demonstrates a certain spirit of humility that God is sure to appreciate. But if you can't even bring yourself to do *that*, then please don't kid yourself—your problem has nothing to do with a lack of faith. It has to do with pride. I'm going to talk more about the whole "faith decision" a little later. But I'm telling you right now, an inability to even take a chance that there's a God by offering up the simplest of prayers is not a good sign that you're open to ever experiencing true happiness.

But let's say you *are* able to at least say good morning to God. In fact, let's even say you're a committed Catholic who goes to church every Sunday. I'll bet there's *still* something you're not doing every morning that you should be—something that could drastically and immediately improve your life. It's called the Morning Offering, and it's a very simple but beautiful prayer that packs an awful lot of punch. Without going into an explanation about the various theological terms used in this formula, I'll just say that, in baseball terminology, this is the equivalent of starting your day with a grand slam. Just print this out on a small piece of paper and put it on your nightstand. Or put it on your smartphone in a place you can access immediately. Then every morning, after giving your first thought to God and after saying an Our Father, repeat these words, giving *yourself* to God:

> *My Lord Jesus Christ, through the Immaculate Heart of Mary, I offer You my prayers, works, joys, and sufferings of this day for all the intentions of Your Sacred Heart, in union with the Holy Sacrifice of the Mass throughout the world, for the salvation of souls, the reparation of sins, the relief of those suffering in Purgatory, the reunion of all Christians, and in particular for the intentions of the Holy Father. Amen.*

Don't be fooled by how short this prayer is. Believe me, it's powerful. By saying it, you'll be aligning yourself with the will of the Creator of the universe and with the Church He founded. You'll be dedicating your whole day to God. And you'll be sanctifying that day before it even begins. You won't even have gotten out of bed, and you'll already be a million miles ahead of most of the population of the planet. That's a heck of a lot to accomplish in just the first few minutes after you've opened your eyes!

You think you might not have time for it, or you might not remember to do it? Come on! I bet you have time to check your social media accounts before you get out of bed, don't you? I bet you remember to check to see how many likes your Instagram post received while you were sleeping. And yet you don't think you have time to say one ten-second prayer to the One who gave you life? Of course you have!

The next thing you *must* do is buy yourself a copy of the New Testament. You know the kind I mean—those small books that can fit practically anywhere, even in your pocket. You can take them to work or on vacation, or you can just leave them on the nightstand next to your bed. You need to get one. Or you need to purchase one of those Bible apps for your smartphone. There are dozens of versions, and they're either free or very cheap. If you don't already have one, get one *now*.

Why? Because you have to start reading it right away, that's why! We're talking about the Word of God. That's something you need to hear. People all over the world whimper and whine about God's "silence." But the fact is that God talks to us in many ways. And nowhere does He speak more clearly and loudly than in Sacred Scripture.

Remember, Christians believe that Jesus Christ *is* God. He wasn't just some holy man. He wasn't just some teacher like Socrates or Confucius or Buddha. He was and is God Almighty in human form. So if you want to see God walking around, you have to read the Gospels. If you want to hear God speaking, you have to read the Gospels. If you want to know the message that God has for the world today and for you personally, you have to read the Gospels.

The bottom line is that you should read a little bit of the New Testament every day. It doesn't have to be a lot. Some people read only one chapter. Some go through the whole Bible from start to finish, every year. I, myself, try to read a page or two every night. Then when I get to the end of the Gospels, I start right back again at the beginning. But you don't have to be so ambitious. For now, just start with a single verse or a single passage a day.

That's one little sentence! Can you handle that?

There used to be a great saying: "No Bible, no breakfast. No Bible, no bed." In other words, you shouldn't have those eggs and bacon in the morning unless you've first nourished your soul with Scripture. You shouldn't lay your head on your pillow at night unless you've first put your day in perspective with the Word of God.

That's a wonderful rule. But for the sake of making things as easy as possible, I would say that you should commit to at least the second part: "No Bible, no bed." If you have to miss reading in the morning, fine (as long as you've said your morning prayer). But you absolutely shouldn't go to sleep at night unless you've read some of the New Testament.

If you do this, not only will you be saying good night to God in a way He truly appreciates, but you'll be nourishing your subconscious mind with God too—and that will bring blessings upon you *as you sleep*. So many people spend the last few minutes of the day rehashing all their problems, all the things that have gone wrong in their lives, all the stressful situations with which they must contend in the days ahead. Then they wonder why they have nightmares and wake up in the morning with knots in their stomachs.

Instead of programming yourself with stress, why not try programming yourself with God's peace?

Now, is this all there is to the spiritual life? Of course not. There's much, much more. There's love of God and neighbor, there's worship, there's self-sacrifice, there's obedience to the Ten Commandments, there's the Holy Eucharist and the other sacraments and the whole life of the Church. And all of it's important. This is just the beginning. But the beginning is oh so critical: talking to God, reading the Scriptures, doing it over and over again until it becomes a part of you; until saying your first prayer in the morning is as natural as taking your first breath—and as necessary; until reading the Bible at night is as automatic as brushing your teeth and putting on your pajamas.

Please don't misunderstand me. I'm not talking here about meaningless repetition or mindless rote. When you open the Gospel and read that verse or that chapter, you should be listening for God to speak to you. You should have an openness to whatever God is telling you. If you're experiencing problems in your marriage or your health or your job, you have to trust that God is going to help you through your reading and your prayer. You have to trust that God is going to use the Bible to bestow abundant graces on you. That openness and that trust and that consistency is something that God is going to reward. But you have to stick with it! You have to do it every day—no excuses.

But you're too tired, you say.

Sorry, do it anyway!

But you're sick with the flu.

Sorry, do it anyway!

But you feel like a hypocrite because you were just sinning.

Sorry, do it anyway!

None of that matters! I don't care what kinds of sins you may have committed. And I don't care if you only just committed them before bedtime. Don't you go to sleep without reading the Bible. Don't worry about "hypocrisy." Just do an about-face, as we discussed earlier. God will help you take care of that in His own time. You're probably not a hypocrite anyway. You're probably just a weak, habitual sinner—like the rest of us. But reading the Bible is your *lifeline*. This is something that will keep you anchored to God, no matter what your emotional mood or sinful setbacks are.

So just do it! Every morning, say a prayer to God immediately upon waking, and every evening read a little bit of the New Testament right before bed. Do these two things without fail—starting *now*. And make a commitment to do them forever.

Till the day you die.

Action Items

- ✓ Print out the morning offering or put it on an easily accessible digital device.
- ✓ Purchase either a hard copy or electronic copy of the New Testament.
- ✓ Before bed tonight, read a verse or two of the New Testament, starting with the Gospel of Matthew.
- ✓ Starting tomorrow morning, say an Our Father the moment you wake up and also pray the Morning Offering.
- ✓ If you are an atheist or an agnostic, every morning for the remainder of this month, sincerely ask God to show you that He exists.

Move!

Okay, you've put God first. Great! That's a huge step in the right direction. You're already far ahead of most of the world. But keeping in mind what we discussed earlier about taking a "full person" approach to life, what's next on the list?

The answer is simple, but once again, it's something that people either don't do enough, or do in mad binges, or do too much of—to the point where it becomes almost a kind of religion of its own. I'm talking about taking care of your body. In particular, I'm talking about physical exercise.

Let's start with the people who do too much. There *is* such a thing as focusing too much on exercise and too much on your health. G. K. Chesterton said that "the mere pursuit of health" for health's sake "always leads to something unhealthy. Physical nature . . . must be enjoyed, not worshipped."[2]

The folks who spend four hours at the gym every day, who eat nothing but organic fruit and nuts, whose best friend is the mirror, and whose biggest holiday of the year is Earth Day have obviously crossed a line. Their main problem—though they don't know it—is

[2] G. K. Chesterton, *Orthodoxy*, chap. 5.

a moral one. They're essentially doing what Chesterton warned against: worshipping nature, specifically, their own bodies. For them, health has become an idol—their highest goal and aspiration in life.

Only health is not supposed to be the highest goal. Christians know that their real home is Heaven and that their life on earth could end at any time. Therefore, we should never cling to our bodies as if they were the most important things in the world. We always have to have our "bags packed" so to speak—because we know we can be "called home" at any moment. Thus, health must always be a secondary goal. It must be regarded as a means to an end, and not the end itself. The true end, or purpose, of life is to be in union with God; to do His will—thereby ensuring not only eternal life in Heaven but also peace and happiness and love right now.

That's the ultimate objective of life. Not good health, not longevity, not the preservation of youth. And so these people who obsess over their bodies and nature to an inordinate degree become "unnatural" themselves. They redefine morality *in terms of health* (often a shortsighted and distorted view of health) and not in terms of God's law or even commonsense ethics. Their priorities are all wrong—and so they usually end up being wrong on a slew of other moral issues as well. For instance, they might come to the conclusion that it's okay for an unwanted pregnancy to be terminated because what's at stake is "the right to reproductive health" and not a baby's life. Or they might think it's acceptable to remove a feeding tube from a brain-damaged young girl for the purpose of starving her because her "quality of mental health" has been compromised to such a degree that her life is no longer "worth" preserving. These folks worship health, and so the paradoxical result is that instead of bringing more life to the world, they become harbingers of death.

But let's put these nature-loving health fanatics aside for the moment. And let's save any discussion about serious societal evils till later. Let's say instead that you've got your priorities in better order. Let's say your problem isn't that you're fixated on your body but rather the opposite—that you're like most people in society who neglect their bodies. Maybe you *really* neglect it. Did you know that's immoral too?

Of course it is. The body is the temple of the Holy Spirit, remember? That's straight from the Bible (1 Cor. 6:19). And doesn't it make sense? If the goal of life is to perform God's will, won't you be able to do that in a more vibrant and perfect way if you have good health? Doesn't it follow logically that if you take care of your body, you'll also have more energy and more mobility and more strength and may even be able to live longer? Won't you therefore be able to do what God wants you to do in the most efficient, effective way possible? And doesn't that translate into helping more people?

That's just common sense. The Eastern religions don't have any monopoly on the "spirituality of health." On the contrary, one of the main tenets of Christianity is that the body has value as well as the soul, but we Christians demonstrate our faith in that belief in a much different way. Unlike the ideal of a sitting or squatting, stationary Buddha, the very essence of Christianity is to be active, energetic, exuberant, and, above all, on the move. Christianity is a religion not only of great emotion—but also of great *motion*. From the very beginning, it has been marching, moving, spreading, and running.

Just read the Gospels. Except when He's praying, Jesus isn't standing still for a minute. He's always on the go, traveling from village to village, healing, teaching, performing miracles. And that activity doesn't end with His death. In the accounts of the Resurrection of Christ, you'll see women running from the empty tomb to find the disciples; you'll see Mary Magdalene running to give Peter the news that she saw the risen Christ; you'll see Peter and John running to the tomb in excitement, almost racing to see who will get there first. There's just a lot of running going on. In fact, the end of the Gospels is filled with physical movement. Peter even dives into the water and swims to the shore like an Olympic athlete when he recognizes Jesus standing there.

And that's not the end of the action. Before Christ ascends into Heaven, He gives the apostles what is known as the Great Commission: "Go therefore and make disciples of all nations" (Matt. 28:19). Notice He doesn't say "sit" and make disciples of all nations, or "stay" and make disciples of all nations. He says *go!* After that command, a period of feverish activity begins. The letters of St. Paul contain an abundant number of words and phrases having to do with athletic competition—"boxing," "strenuous exercise," "striving for mastery," "running a race with perseverance," "winning," to name just a few. In his Second Letter to Timothy, he famously writes: "I have fought the good fight, I have finished the race, I have kept the faith" (4:7).

None of these metaphors is an accident. The whole point of Christianity is to advance, to be on the march. When you have good news, the last thing you want to do is sit down and keep it to yourself. Rather, you want to share it with everyone. Especially *this* good news. The message of the Gospels is that death is *not* the end of life, that suffering is *not* the end of the story, that there *is* a God, that He *does* love us, and that we're going to live forever in Heaven if we embrace that truth with faith. That's not the kind of information you keep secret.

Even the main symbol of Christianity is a metaphor for action. Look at the Cross and compare it with the traditional symbols of Eastern religions such as Buddhism—which are always circular in design. Eastern religions are all about looking inward, meditating on oneself, or about the infinite circle of life. Christianity, on the other hand, is all about dynamic movement, and so its symbol is made up of two bold, crossed lines extending outward to all points of the globe—north, south, east, and west. Ultimately, Christianity is a faith of joyful action, and if you believe in it and want to spread it, it's important that you yourself are able to take action with energy and decisiveness.

Now, let me take a second to clarify something. I know there are people out there who are elderly and sick and unable to get around. I've just pointed out the connection between Christianity and motion, but I don't want anyone to get the wrong idea. No matter what stage of life you're at, no matter how sick or handicapped you are, you can *always* do God's will. Even if you're stuck on a hospital bed with all kinds of tubes coming out of you, you can still be a shining example to others of how to face suffering with courage and faith. And like the battery of a car, which doesn't move at all but gives power to the entire vehicle, you can be motionless yourself and still move the whole world through the power of your prayers. Every human being, from conception till natural death, has more dignity than a billion soulless galaxies. A person's worth is not decreased one iota because he or she can't move. That's been a bedrock belief of Christianity for two thousand years.

But I'm not talking about that here. I'm assuming that you're *not* at death's door. I'm assuming that even if you're old and sick, you still have some energy left in your body—some ability to move. And if that's the case, then everything I'm saying applies to you. We all know how important movement is. In fact, there's not a health book or program in the world that doesn't insist on the need for weekly aerobic activity. It's just essential for your physical well-being—and your mental and emotional well-being as well.

That's one of the reasons people today are so unhappy. So many of us live sedentary lives. We get up in the morning and sit in our cars on the way to work; then we sit at our desks for eight hours; then we drive back home and sit at our dinner tables to eat; then we sit in front of the TV and watch our favorite sitcom or we sit in front of the computer and play video games or fool around with social media; then we finally go to bed and lie there for another eight hours before getting up and starting the whole process over again. And we do this every week for years on end. Then we wonder why we've got the energy, physique, and emotional outlook of a slug worm!

Look, I'm no doctor, but I'll tell you something now that's as true as anything you'll ever read in a health magazine or psychology journal. The body needs activity as much as a motor needs oil and fuel. So if you want your life to change for the better, you've got to stop being a couch potato! You've got to get *moving*. Regular movement improves everything. Your energy levels. Your stress levels. Your ability to sleep. Your ability to digest. Your ability to burn calories. Your body weight. Your breathing. Your bone density. Your blood pressure. Your circulation. Moving makes your heart and lungs stronger. It slows down age-related muscle loss and fragility. It makes all your systems work more efficiently. It improves your cognitive function. It decreases the chances of a cardiac event by 50 percent. It improves your muscular and joint stability, balance, flexibility, range of motion, and coordination. It causes your body to release powerful chemicals called endorphins, which make you feel more relaxed and elated and also make your immune system more resistant to sickness and disease. It helps your body to quickly change emotional states in ways we don't fully understand. Sometimes just shaking your whole body out and briskly walking around the block or jogging in place can do wonders for relieving the daily doldrums or even more serious problems with depression.

Ask any mechanic: If you want to make sure your car stays running properly, you've got to drive it regularly. You can't keep it locked up in the garage all year. If you do that, when you attempt to start it, you're going to hear nothing but clicks. And if you do manage to get it going, it's very liable to have serious problems—many more problems than if you had taken it out for a short spin every few days. Machines are built to be used; that's what keeps them functioning. And that goes for every kind of machine—including the human body.

There's just no way around it. You've got to move, move, move, and you've got to keep moving. In fact, when you stop moving completely, that's when you know you're dead! Isn't that right? Isn't that one of the main characteristics of something that's dead—the total cessation of movement? That's why moving isn't just something related to health and fitness. It's something sacred. It's something holy. It's the most visible sign of life—God's first and greatest blessing to us. That's why I'm including a discussion about it in this book.

The good news is that this isn't hard to do. This isn't about training for a decathlon or subjecting your body to great stress. Do you know how much movement is required for optimal health? *Thirty to sixty minutes, three or four days a week.* That's it! Between 90 and 240 minutes total! And it makes no difference how you break that total time up or what kind of movement you do—running, walking, swimming, cycling, general aerobics work—all of it is good.

Nor should the movement be too strenuous. The purpose of those thirty to sixty minutes is just to get your heart rate up a little and to keep it up. In fact, you should be able to carry on a normal conversation as you're moving without having to catch your breath—without huffing and puffing. If you can't do that, then you're going too fast.

Remember, we're not talking about a weight-loss plan here. We're not talking about a fitness program. We're not talking about burning calories. We're not talking about a way to build muscle. We're not talking about a way to reverse cancer. We're talking about a simple thing you can do to significantly improve your physical, mental, emotional, and even spiritual health, immediately—no matter what your condition.

Can you do more? Of course you can. Of course it's in your best interests if you can add some strength training to your weekly routine. Of course it will benefit your body if you can do brief high-intensity workouts on a regular basis. Of course it's wonderful to have an active, sporting lifestyle. All of these things might give you more energy, increase the quality of your life, and even—possibly—help you to live longer. But none of them is strictly necessary—not for our purposes, anyway. What we're talking about here is the *minimum* you can do to get the *maximum* results.

Do you know that if you did nothing else for your health except go outside into the fresh air and sunshine and walk for thirty minutes, four times a week, and did it consistently for a decade, you'd be much healthier, overall, than 90 percent of the people who take vitamins and minerals and a whole battery of supplements and who binge on exercise fads and crazy diets but then stop after a few years because of injuries or emotional problems or family problems or a thousand other things? I, myself, try to walk one hour a day. I like to pace around my home, so it's easy for me. I've been doing it for years, and I've always had robust health and abundant energy.

The key is consistency. This whole book is really about consistency—doing the simplest, most basic things, but doing them over and over until they become part of who you are. Sure, it's easy to get motivated by something you read or hear and then go to the gym a few times. But it's quite another thing to find a way to consistently exercise even when the weather is bad, or when you're feeling depressed, or when you can't pay your bills, or when the kids are screaming, or when you feel as if it's a waste of time because you've been eating so badly. That's when you really find out what you're made of.

You have to approach this problem as if it were a military campaign. You have to look at your week with a cold, objective eye and ask yourself a series of questions. Where can you find three thirty-minute blocks—or six fifteen-minute blocks? How can you carve out the time, given all the other obligations in your life? And in addition to these solid blocks of time, how can you increase your *general level of activity* every day? How can you avoid regular and prolonged sedentary periods? How can you reverse the "couch potato syndrome"?

For instance, do you have any health-conscious friends you can make plans with? Are there any outdoor sports you can take up? Do you have a dog you can walk, and is there a playground the two of you can go to? If you shop at the grocery store or the mall every week, can you park your car farther away from the entrance in order to guarantee yourself a nice walk? Is there a coffee shop you can walk to in fifteen minutes from where you live or work? Can you take the stairs more often instead of using an escalator or an elevator? Can you take up a hobby that involves regular movement, such as gardening or golf? Would it help you to get one of those apps for your smartphone that counts steps—and then aim for five thousand to ten thousand steps per day? If you're able to afford a gym membership, how are you going to deal with the boredom of jogging or walking or biking on an exercise machine?

Can you listen to audiobooks or music? Can you spend the time praying? How about the Rosary?

Do you know that if you got yourself some rosary beads, put them in a pouch, carried the pouch in your pocket, and prayed the Rosary every single day *while walking*, it would give you over *an hour and a half* of exercise for the week? It takes only about fifteen minutes to say the Rosary. Multiply that by seven days, and you've got all the movement you need for the week! If you add to that the Chaplet of Divine Mercy—which takes about five minutes to pray—you've got another thirty-five minutes of walking per week. That's physiological and spiritual dynamite!

But it's cold outside, you say. So what? Pace around your house. Go from room to room, meditating on the life of Christ while exercising. That's what the Franciscan friars have been doing for hundreds of years. Who cares if some people think you look silly? You'll be moving your body to improve your health, and you'll be making the experience profoundly meaningful for your spirit too.

That's just one idea. There are plenty others. But you get the point. You really have to think hard about how you're going to tackle this problem. You have to find a way to make this time of movement not only doable but *enjoyable*. Remember, this isn't just about your body. It's about your whole being. More important, it's about your relationship with God and your ability to do what He wants you to do more perfectly and effectively. If you're more vibrant and energetic, He's going to utilize you to help Him in a greater variety of ways. That's serious business—a lot more serious than just trying to lose a few pounds. Don't you agree?

The bottom line is this: If you're not feeling particularly good about your life—or if you're just feeling a little sluggish or sad—try to snap out of it for a second. Stop thinking all those hopeless thoughts! Remember that motion and emotion are intimately connected. Get off the couch *now*. The couch is your enemy. The couch will kill you. The couch is not only body-destroying but soul-destroying. If you don't get off it soon, someone's going to come and throw dirt on you! Instead of sitting around doing nothing, take a break and go outside. Get to where there's some daylight. Shake yourself out. Walk around the block. Try to figure out how you're going to execute the simple plan I've suggested here—and how you're going to stick to it.

In other words, try taking a lesson from the early Christians. Get off your butt and *move*!

Action Items

✓ Look at your weekly schedule and map out your "Campaign to Move." Write it down, commit to executing it, and start today.

Bringing Order out of Chaos

Here's another spiritual principle that has far-ranging implications—especially in terms of helping us to take control of our lives. From the beginning of the Bible to the end, one thing is extraordinarily clear: *God is a God of order.*

The very first thing God did after He created the universe was to organize it—to separate light from darkness, to divide the water and the land, to bring clarity to the chaos. Now, of course these images aren't scientific. They aren't meant to be. Sacred Scripture should never be confused with a high school physics textbook. The point of Scripture is to present the deeper, underlying truth about life. And the tremendous truth being conveyed in the opening pages of the book of Genesis has to do with the nature of God.

God is simple in substance. God is purity. God is clarity. God is order. That's the truth to get into our heads.

And when God became man in the person of Jesus Christ, He demonstrated those same characteristics again. Christ came into the world to perform a certain mission—the salvation of humanity. And He did it with extraordinary speed, order, and effectiveness. He was born in a very simple manner and then spent the first thirty years of His life in total, hidden quiet, preparing Himself. Once He began, it took Him only three short years to accomplish His objective. In three years, He turned the whole world upside down—and it hasn't been the same since. Three years! That's efficiency for you! That's God.

When Christ died on the Cross and rose from the dead, He did something else that showed this characteristic. On that first Easter morning, when the apostles discovered His empty tomb, they noticed something very interesting. They noticed that the burial cloth that had been used to cover Jesus' face was rolled up neatly in the corner. Such a tiny detail. But what significance! It means that when Jesus Christ rose from the dead, the first thing He did was to tidy up! The first thing He did was to put everything in its proper place—to clean His tomb before leaving it forever.

And of course, that's to be expected. After all, Christ is God. And God's nature is to be orderly and clean.

Now compare this with the way you conduct your own life. I'll bet you're not always very Godlike when it comes to orderliness, are you? I'll bet that if you took inventory of your entire life, you'd find quite a bit of *disorder*.

But let's go deeper. Let's try to understand the root of disorder. What we've got to keep in mind here is that the thing most contrary to God is *sin*. The act of sinning is simply the act of turning away from God, right? Well, when we turn away from God—and then move in the opposite direction—what invariably happens is that we begin to take on qualities that are *different* from God; qualities that are *contrary* to God; qualities that are *opposite* to God. And that includes disorder.

Sin, by its very nature, is division. It's disintegration. It's a falling apart—a breakdown of order. When we're not acting in line with God's will for us, that kind of disintegration happens to us on the inside—in our souls. There's an internal collapse that's not immediately perceptible to the people around us; an invisible chaos that we're sometimes not even aware of, even though we usually *feel* it in the form of unhappiness.

The good news is that what happens to us on the inside is sure to turn up on the outside—if we give it enough time. In other words, when our internal lives are messy, our exterior lives eventually become messy too. I say this is good news because if there's a visible manifestation of the internal chaos, at least it can be a sign to us that something needs to change.

What happens when things break down morally and spiritually for us is that our *whole life* breaks down as well. And I mean this in the most literal way. It's not just that our relationships break down or our finances break down—though these things certainly can occur. I mean that our homes and our offices and our cars break down too. They all get sloppy. They all get dirty. Disorder prevails. Chaos reigns.

Now don't misunderstand me. I'm not saying that if you've got a messy house, it's proof you've been sinning. Not at all. There are lots of reasons people are disorganized. It might be because they have bad habits. It might be because they were raised in chaotic environments. It might be that they're feeling depressed. It might be that they have a house full of kids. A breakdown in morality isn't the only cause of a breakdown in order. But that doesn't change the fact that there is a mystical connection between the interior state of your soul and the exterior state of your environment. What you do in one area affects the other.

And this is the point we need to understand. When we finally become tired of the chaos and emotional turmoil that often accompany a spiritual breakdown, it's almost instinctive for us to want to physically clean up. No matter what the root problem is, we know deep down that we have to start eliminating the clutter. And so it's common to hear people say they've had enough and are finally going to force themselves to clean their closet or their garage or whatever.

Sometimes people will poke fun at this natural inclination. They'll say that it's mere avoidance; that it's like "putting a Band-Aid on cancer." That because we don't want to take on the more painful, deeper problems in our marriage and our job and our finances; we instead tend to work on other, less challenging tasks, like cleaning the closet. We do this, they say, in order to fool ourselves into believing that we're really making progress, to *distract* ourselves from the main problems of life, to simply make ourselves feel good. In other words, some people think we're just wasting our time by cleaning up.

But guess what? They're wrong! They're missing the point completely. They're missing the whole spiritual significance of disorder. And so naturally they end up in a muddle themselves.

Sure, if cleaning up were the only thing a person ever did to combat his or her problems, it would qualify as a distraction. But it's not meant to be the only thing. It's meant to be a step. A step in the right direction. A step to build momentum. And we've already talked about how important momentum is.

Straightening up and putting things in order is always a good thing to do. The reason is that it's a sign you're trying to be in union with God—who, as we said, *is* order. No matter what the problem, cleaning your desk or your office or your house is necessary because it's an attempt to make your work and living space more Godlike. It's an attempt to conform those spaces to God's nature. And that's never a mistake.

The same goes for cleaning yourself. Have you ever noticed that when things start to go really wrong in your life, all you want to do is stay in bed? When you're feeling lousy, it's difficult to even get washed and dressed and groomed in the morning. In addition to the other problems you have, there always seems to be an extra temptation to indulge in the sin of sloth—better known as laziness—especially with regard to your appearance and your schedule. Why do you think that is?

I'll tell you the answer—and I know I keep hammering home this same point—it's because *everything is connected*. The body, mind, and spirit are all tied together. What you do to one affects the other two and the whole. If you're moving toward God—that is, trying to do *His* will, play by *His* rules, follow *His* map—then everything else in your life will start to "align" itself too, eventually resulting in greater peace and happiness. If you're moving away from God—that is, trying to do *your* will, play by *your* rules, and follow *your* map—then everything else in your life will start to get chaotic and confused, not to mention depressing. And that's going to result in lethargy.

One of the best ways to combat this deterioration is to systematically eliminate the chaos from your life. You've heard the old saying "Cleanliness is next to godliness"? Well, it's truer than you ever imagined. In fact, it's one of the most important spiritual truths in the universe. And it's time we all tried to make it part of our lifestyle.

But hold on, you say. This doesn't make sense. There are plenty of movie stars, rock stars, and billionaires who are living morally bankrupt lives but seem to be quite content and quite organized. They flaunt their bad behavior publicly and bash Christianity every chance they get, and yet they always look so beautiful and pristine and fashionable. Surely their lives are orderly. Surely they're happy. But how can that be? Have these folks managed to find some loophole in the spiritual law?

No, they haven't! The truth is that they may seem happy, but they're not. Don't believe it! If you look past the glamour and glitz and makeup and plastic surgery, you'll quickly see all the tangled confusion of their lives—all the broken marriages, all the lawsuits, all the divided property, all the scattered children, all the tax problems, all the drug and alcohol problems, all the overdoses, all the infidelities, all the depression, all the suicides, all the *mess*.

None of it is clean and orderly. None of it is truly joyful. Remember what Christ said about the Pharisees. He called them "whitewashed tombs, which outwardly appear beautiful, but within ... are full of dead men's bones and all uncleanness" (Matt. 23:27).

You can't allow that to be you. This book is not about becoming "whitewashed tombs." You may be a weak and sinful human being, but you at least have to try to do God's will. You at least have to try to be clean—on the inside *and* the outside. That's what makes all the difference.

So here's the bottom line: You need to take a quick survey of your life and then make a list of all the areas that need to be straightened out. Then you need to start cleaning up—one mess at a time. First your desk, then your office, then your e-mails, then your computer files, then your kitchen, then your garage, then your vehicle, then your closets, then your clothes. In whichever order you prefer. I know this can be a challenge—especially if you have young kids running around the house, leaving havoc in their wake. But you have to try!

And if you happen to be depressed, you have to force yourself to make your bed in the morning. You have to push yourself to take that extra-long shower. You have to make an effort to dress nicely. Not fancy. Not expensive. You don't need to wear Armani suits or Ferragamo shoes. This isn't about being extravagant. It's about being clean and neat and well put together—no matter what your emotional or physical condition.

Then you need to try to clean up your head. Your mind can get more cluttered than any room in your home because there are an infinite number of things you can put there. Did you ever see one of those computer screens that have hundreds of windows opened at the same time? Doesn't your brain feel like that sometimes? Well, it's time to start closing those windows and shutting down those open programs. Do you know how to do that? By focusing. By taking some quiet time every day and concentrating on God. The secular world calls it meditation. But Christians call it prayer.

Please don't get stressed over any of this. There's no need to do everything at once. I don't care if I sound like a broken record, but slow and steady wins the race. What we're interested in here is long-lasting change—not a mere spring cleaning. Little by little, start to bring your life under the sovereignty of God's order.

Then just watch the results. Within a few weeks, you'll see an amazing transformation take place. I guarantee that as all the clutter begins to clear, the path leading to true peace and happiness will become a whole lot easier for you to see—and to follow.

Action Items

✓ Map out your "Campaign to Organize." Make a list of all the things that need to be cleaned up in your life, big and small. Pick one item on the list—an easy one—and start with that *today*.

Hit the Reset Button — Fast!

For the past week we've been talking about ways you can quickly take control of your life—simple things you can do to help break bad habits and reverse unproductive patterns of behavior.

Right now, I'm going to give you something extremely powerful that you can do whenever you stray from the right path or things get chaotic in your life. I call it the "24-Hour Reset Fast," and I've used it myself for many years with extraordinary results.

"Fasting" is defined as abstaining from food or drink for certain periods of time. As we'll see later, fasting can have a much broader meaning, as well. You can fast from any activity—like going on social media or watching TV or listening to music or shopping—and those acts of self-denial can be very beneficial in developing your willpower. But for the purposes of this chapter, we're going to focus on fasting from food and beverages other than water.

Now, fasting is something that's been around for thousands of years. Catholics and many other Christians fast on Ash Wednesday and Good Friday; Jews fast on Yom Kippur and other major holidays; Muslims fast during Ramadan, the ninth month of the Islamic calendar; Hindus fast during the month of Śravaṇa; many Buddhists fast on their major holidays as well as every day from noon until the following dawn.

Not only do all the major world religions advocate fasting as a means of spiritual discipline, preparation, and purification, but nonreligious people recognize its value too. Fasting is often prescribed before medical procedures and surgeries, and it's used to treat various degenerative diseases and other kinds of debilitating conditions. Indeed, fasting is currently quite popular. If you look online, you'll see hundreds of enthusiasts talking about intermittent fasting, time-restricted eating, wet fasts, dry fasts, calorie-restricted fasts, nutrient-restricted fasts, three-day fasts, five-day fasts, seasonal fasts, and so on.

The reason fasting is all the rage today is because of its reputed health benefits. Studies show that fasting can decrease your glucose levels and increase your insulin sensitivity, and this, in turn, can positively impact all the organs and systems of your body. Fasting can improve your immune system and your brain function. It can kick-start ketosis and help you to lose weight quickly. It can cleanse your body of toxins. It can help prevent or reverse some forms of diabetes. It can give you greater metabolic stability and flexibility. Fasting for a few days can even bring about a physiological process known as autophagy, which causes the body to eliminate dead cells, recycle damaged cells, and grow healthier new cells. Autophagy is essentially a biological "spring cleaning," in which the body washes, purifies, strengthens, and rebuilds itself from the inside out. There's even some evidence that periodic fasting—with its resultant autophagy—can increase longevity.

When religious and nonreligious groups agree on the value of a specific activity—and they don't agree on much of anything nowadays—you can bet there's something to it. But do you know the most convincing proof that fasting is beneficial? It's that no one stands to make any profit from it! Think about it. Everyone in the health industry is selling something. The mainstream medical community, the pharmaceutical companies, the alternative-medicine industry, the integrative-medicine industry, the supplement industry, the juicing and green-drink industry—they're all making a great deal of money from their myriad products and services. But nobody makes anything when people stop eating or drinking. Common sense tells you that fasting must be so powerful that it's impossible to ignore, despite its relative inability to generate revenue.

We don't have time here for a comprehensive discussion of the health benefits of fasting. Besides, I'm not your doctor, and this book isn't about extending your life. It's about making your life better. That's where the 24-Hour Reset Fast comes in. It will make your life better, almost instantaneously.

For people who have never done it, the thought of fasting for twenty-four hours can be horrifying. In fact, I can already hear some readers shrieking: "You mean I can't have my breakfast, lunch, and dinner? You mean I can't have my favorite snacks? You mean I can't have my—gulp—coffee?"

That's right. At the end of this chapter, we're going to pick a start time that's right for your schedule, and beginning then, you won't be able to have any of those things for twenty-four hours. No food, no alcohol, no soda, no fruit juice, no coffee. Just good old H_2O.

Why would anyone undertake such a fast, aside from its theoretical health benefits?

Listen, my friend, you're in the middle of a self-transformation program. Presumably, the reason is that something is wrong with your life. Maybe something is missing. Maybe something has gone off-track. Maybe you're depressed. Maybe you're overwhelmed. Maybe you're trapped by compulsive behavior. Maybe you're in a state of despair because you think nothing will ever change. Maybe you're simply not very content and you recognize that you could be doing a lot better. Whatever the reason, the point of this book is to help you take control of your life and fix it.

So let me ask you a question. When your cell phone or your tablet or your laptop computer or your TV or any device you own starts to go haywire and refuses to work properly, what's one of the first things you do to fix it?

You turn it off and on again, right? You restart it. You reset it. Sometimes that's all it needs to begin working again.

Well, how do you go about resetting yourself when *you* aren't working properly? How do you mimic the act of turning yourself off and on again?

This is the way! By fasting for twenty-four hours!

What you have to understand is that so many of your problems are the result of your weakened will. Over the years, your will has lost much of its innate power. The world and all its glittering attractions have been working hard to erode it. In fact, the world is always trying to brainwash you. It's always trying to get you to eat certain foods, drink certain beverages, buy certain products, wear certain clothes, use certain perfumes, watch certain programs, read certain books, vote for certain candidates, believe certain principles, accept certain "facts," become addicted to certain activities, and on and on, *ad nauseam*.

In order to persuade you to do these things, the world has many effective tools at its disposal: advertisements via social media, television, and radio, propaganda via the entertainment industry, indoctrination via the education system, biased reporting via the mass media, ideologically driven laws and court decisions via the government. All of these methods are employed with the most sophisticated use of words, sounds, and images designed to tap into your deepest physiological and emotional desires.

This isn't some half-baked conspiracy theory. It's the truth. The world knows that human beings crave instant gratification—and that's what it's always offering us. That's why we all must stand guard at the door of our minds; otherwise, the world will break through and fill us with thousands of dangerous toxins. It's so easy today to become poisoned and brainwashed and addicted. It's so easy to become puppets—the kind of puppets we talked about on Day 1 of this program.

We're always saying yes to the world because the world is so cunning. In fact, we're so used to saying yes that it's hard to tell how many of our troubles are the results of the bad things that happen to us and how many are caused by the poor habits we've picked up from constantly saying yes to the endless barrage of seductive images we're subjected to. In other words, it's hard to tell how much of our suffering is self-inflicted.

And why do we say yes to the world? Because our willpower is no longer strong enough to say no.

But when you go on a twenty-four-hour fast you do indeed say *no* to the world. You say *no* to instant gratification. You say *no* to your body. You say *no* to your emotions. You say *no* to your whole psychology. You completely interrupt your usual self-indulgent way of interacting with the world, and it's this radical "pattern interrupt" that's equivalent to "restarting" your computer when it's not working.

By giving up all food and drink except water for twenty-four hours, you might not be saying no to shopping or social media or TV or cigarettes or porn or gambling or other kinds of worldly temptations, but you *are* saying no to something incredibly desirable and necessary, a craving that springs from your deepest instinct—your instinct to survive. When you say no to eating, it does something to your body by purifying it; it does something to your will by strengthening it; it does something to your brain by teaching it that you *do* have self-control; it does something to your soul by acting as a form of penance for bad behavior and a form of preparation for better behavior in the future.

This last benefit is especially important. Just look through the Bible to see how essential fasting has always been as a means of preparing God's people to do great things. For example, Moses fasted before ascending Mount Sinai to receive the Ten Commandments (Exod. 34:28); Elijah fasted in order to escape the evil queen Jezebel (1 Kings 19:8); Esther fasted in order to save the Jewish people from destruction (Esther 4:16); Daniel fasted in order to understand the mysterious vision God had given him (Dan. 10:3); Anna the prophetess fasted before seeing the Baby Jesus in the temple (Luke 2:37); the apostles fasted after Jesus' Ascension in order to help them fulfill the Great Commission: to make disciples of all nations (Acts 13:2–3); St. Paul fasted in order to endure all his hardships—to fight the good fight, finish the race and keep the faith (2 Tim. 4:7).

And of course, Our Lord fasted too. Before Jesus was tempted by the devil and before He began His public ministry, He fasted for forty days and forty nights in the wilderness (Matt. 4:2).

Fasting is serious business. It's literally power from Heaven.

You might not be a great prophet or saint from the Bible, but right now you're on a holy mission too. You're on a journey of self-renewal and self-transformation, and you need all the help you can get. Fasting helps your soul in so many ways. It produces humility. It demonstrates sorrow for sins. It helps you to discern God's will. It clears a pathway to following that will by detaching you from the distracting things of the world. Most importantly, fasting is a powerful form of prayer.

The bottom line is that you need to do it, starting today! And here's how.

After dinner tonight, you're going to note the exact time that you finish eating. That's the time you're going to have your next meal tomorrow night. Thus, if you finish your last bite of chicken and your last sip of soda at 7:00 p.m., you're not going to have another morsel of food or another drink of anything other than water until 7:00 p.m. tomorrow night.

For the remainder of the evening, you're not going to consume anything. When you get up tomorrow, say an extra prayer for strength, and then don't ingest anything except water until the twenty-four-hour period is up.

Including coffee!

Naturally, if you need to take certain medications with a bit of food, you can do that. But just the minimum (like a few teaspoons of yogurt) and only if you have to. Likewise, if you have an eating disorder or a health problem that makes a twenty-four-hour fast medically unsafe, you don't have to do it. As I said, I'm not your physician. I'm a friend who's trying to give you the best advice on turning over a new leaf in life. I'm not here to countermand your doctor's orders. So, if you have a *legitimate* reason for not fasting, it's fine to make some other sacrifice instead. But most people—young, old, sick, or healthy—are perfectly capable of going a day without food. Your body can handle it; it's your will that's the problem.

I try to do this kind of fast every few months. In fact, I usually fast a little more than twenty-four hours. After I have my final meal before fasting, I'll try not to eat for at least thirty-six hours. I'll go to sleep the first night without eating after dinner, then I'll go the entire next day without eating. Then I'll go to sleep again on an empty stomach. The first meal I have to "break my fast" won't be till breakfast the following morning.

That's *two nights* while fasting. Talk about a pattern interrupt! Talk about a way to obliterate compulsions! Talk about a way to strengthen your will! Talk about a way to fight worldly temptations! Talk about a way to take back control of your life!

Now if, for some reason, you can't start the fast tonight because you have a breakfast or lunch engagement scheduled for tomorrow, look at your calendar and see when the earliest possible day to begin would be. It shouldn't be Sunday because Sunday is the Lord's Day. It's a day for resting, relaxing, and celebrating. But can you fast on Monday or Tuesday?

The important thing is that you do it *soon*. The two most important weeks of this program are coming up. You're going to be doing some dramatic, challenging, and life-changing things in the next fourteen days. And like those biblical prophets of old, you've got to adequately prepare yourself.

I know that what I'm asking isn't easy. In fact, the 24-Hour Reset Fast is more difficult than the standard "one meal and two snacks" fast that the Catholic Church allows on certain holy days during Lent. This fast is stricter. But it's also more powerful and transformative. We said at the beginning of this program that many people live their lives like sleeping puppets. Well, this fast has the power to throw a bucket of cold water in your face! It can rouse you from your slumber. It can cut the strings you've been dancing on since you were a child. And for some of you, it can even be a way to begin the process of breaking your chains.

Yes, chains.

Chains are what bind slaves, right? Well, many of us are slaves and don't know it. We're slaves to our bodies, our passions, our habits, our compulsions, our addictions, our sins, our hunger for worldly things. We've been slaves for so long that our chains seem natural to us. They're no longer even repugnant, as they should be. And yet, until we break free of them, we can never attain true peace and happiness. St. Paul said that after much labor, he was finally able to make his body a slave to him (1 Cor. 9:27). *That's* the goal we have to set for ourselves. And the best way to start is with this twenty-four-hour fast.

Trust me, it will make a huge difference in your life. So get going and take control—fast!

Action Items

- ✓ Begin your 24-Hour Reset Fast immediately following dinner tonight. Note the time you finish eating. That's the time you can break your fast tomorrow. Remember, you should not consume any food or beverages other than water during the fast.
- ✓ If you are unable to begin tonight, schedule the fast for the earliest possible day, other than Sunday.
- ✓ If you choose to do a thirty-six-hour fast, then your first meal following the fast should be breakfast the day after tomorrow. The meal should be something light and easy to digest, like coffee or tea with yogurt or a smoothie. Check online for the best options.
- ✓ Please note that if you are medically unable to perform a twenty-four-hour water-only fast, do your best to cut down on food for that period, and choose something else to sacrifice as well. Remember, the point of this fast is that it should be difficult enough to exercise and strengthen your will. So don't be easy on yourself!

Controlling Your Rudder

I'd like you to try an experiment. Open your left hand right now and examine your palm. Look at the line going in a zigzag pattern, up and down, up and down. Can you see the M shape formed by the creases in your skin? Sometimes it's a little difficult to make out, but it's there. Everyone has it. Now do the same with your right hand. With your palm open, can you see the M there, right in the middle?

Do you know what the old mystics used to do—the old hermits and monks of the Middle Ages? Every morning, before they began their day, they would look at their two outstretched palms—at the two Ms carved into their hands—and they would meditate on the Latin words *Memento mori*: "Remember you will die!"

Do you think that's morbid? I don't. I call that perspective. I call that wisdom. Let's be honest. No matter how fit you are or how good your genetics, nobody has any guarantee of longevity. You can be the healthiest person in the world, and you can still get hit by a bus. It's impossible to say enough times, but the same God who gave you the morning doesn't promise you the evening. If there was one truth I could drill into people's heads, it would be that. Not because I'm cynical or fatalistic. Quite the contrary; I try to be upbeat about everything. But that's not the same as denying reality. To be a Christian doesn't mean you check your brain at the door. God gave us our brains for a reason: to use them; to recognize and accept certain facts. And the fact is, you can die at *any* time. Therefore, you have to be prepared at *all* times. As the saying goes, nobody gets out of this life alive. So you always have to have your bags packed. You always have to be in a state of mental, emotional, and spiritual *readiness*. That's not being cynical—it's being intelligent.

Now, does that mean you have to live in fear? Of course not! All I'm saying is that you can't afford to blindly waste years on activities that get you nowhere and don't add one iota to your real happiness. And that's what people do all the time. They waste whole decades of their lives. Then they get old or sick, and finally, when they see that the end is in sight, *then* they start spending more time on matters of real consequence—on spiritual matters, moral matters, matters having to do with their eternal soul.

Which is why I want to give you a shortcut now—a way to save time or make up for time that has already been lost. What I'm about to tell you is very important, and I don't want you to think I'm exaggerating for the sake of effect. You won't read it in most self-improvement books or even spiritual books. And yet, if you put this shortcut into practice, I can practically guarantee you that you'll eliminate 80 percent of your emotional and spiritual problems—and probably most of your other faults as well. That's a big promise, I know. But it's true. It has to do with the way we communicate.

St. James, who was an apostle of Christ and one of His closest friends, made the following statement in a famous epistle he wrote:

> *Any man among you who is perfect in speech is a perfect man.* (see James 3:2)

The profound shortcut that God has to offer you is this: If you guard your speech closely and somehow manage to control your tongue, you will consequently control everything else in your life. *Everything.*

What you've got to understand is that the tongue is exactly like the rudder of a ship. You know what the rudder does? It steers the ship; it controls the ship. Now, compared with the size of a ship itself, the rudder is very small. In fact, you can't even see it because it's under water. And yet, when it moves in a certain direction, the whole ship obeys its command and moves with it. It doesn't matter how fierce the winds may be or how high the seas are or how much power is being exerted by the engines; the ship goes wherever that little rudder tells it to go.

Well, that's the same effect the tongue has on the human person. It's our rudder. It's what steers us. It may be small and unseen, but the power it has over what we do and how we act and where we go is incredible. Control the rudder, control the ship. Tame your tongue, tame yourself. It's that simple.

Unfortunately, the reverse is also true. If you fail to control your tongue, you become just like a ship with a broken rudder. You drift aimlessly—or even worse, you crash into other ships or into the dock or the shore. People who don't discipline their tongues go through life destroying everything in their wake. Eventually they become shipwrecked and sink into a sea of their own misery—misery brought about because of the way they've managed to alienate everyone around them.

You know this is true! How many things have you said in your life that you wish you could take back now? Especially all those stupid things said in anger. I can tell you from my own experience that there are things I said thirty years ago that literally make me cringe when I recall them now. Three decades ago—and they still cause me pain!

As one spiritual writer said, human beings have learned to conquer all kinds of harsh environments on the earth and under the sea and even in outer space—but we can't seem to conquer our own tongues. Why?

It goes back again to perspective. Most people today who have poisonous tongues—tongues that spread anger and rumors and gossip and scandal and lies—have completely lost sight of perspective. They spend their lives "majoring in the minors" and, as Richard Carlson said in his best-selling book, "sweating the small stuff."

Those medieval mystics were right. In fact, they had another great Latin saying: *Quid hoc ad aeternitatem.* "What is this in light of eternity?" In other words, why do we get so angry and upset about our problems, when nothing really matters in comparison with the big picture—the picture that involves death and judgment and Heaven and Hell?

We see a little child in a department store crying because his father won't buy him a certain toy. The child is moaning and screaming, all because he's not getting what he wants. At that moment, he's really experiencing a tragedy. He's dying inside because he isn't getting that toy. The other people in the store might be amused at the scene and even laugh. Why? Because they know how unimportant that toy really is. They've lived a little. They have mortgages. They have marriages. They have bills. They have people in their lives whom they've loved and lost. They know what real tragedy is. And they laugh to see a child throwing a temper tantrum over something as meaningless as a toy. In other words, they've gained some perspective.

Well, guess what? The saints in Heaven are laughing at us! We throw temper tantrums all the time because we don't get what we want. Our spouses don't give us the support we need; our children don't give us the appreciation we deserve; our boss doesn't give us the pay raise we've earned; the clerk behind the counter doesn't give us the respect we're due.

They're not giving us the toys we want! Yes, in the light of eternity, those things are all just toys.

You don't think so? One day you might. One day (Heaven forbid), if you were to come out of the doctor's office having just been given the news that the tumor they found is malignant and nothing more can be done, and you were to walk onto the sunny street and see a cabdriver screaming expletives at the car in front of him for not moving fast enough, and a child crying because his ice-cream cone has fallen on the sidewalk, and a woman yelling at her husband for who knows what reason—then you would understand what true perspective is. Then you would understand why deeply spiritual people of every generation and every walk of life—especially those who have known the incomparable peace of Christ—have always seemed so calm and quiet and free from anxiety. It's because they know the answer to the question: *What is this in light of eternity?*

But then again, maybe you're one of those fortunate people who are serene by nature—who would never think of uttering a nasty word. I envy you! I happen to be an Italian American from New York City. I don't like stereotypes, but I have to admit, some of us here have a tendency to express our emotions in ways that are a bit unproductive and uncharitable. We have difficulty with our volume control. We understand the challenge of keeping calm.

But maybe you're not like that. Maybe you have the disposition of an angel. Maybe you're a soft-spoken Midwesterner. Or a friendly Southerner. Or a strong but silent Texan. Or a polite and proper Englishman—I'm really letting the stereotypes fly now! Does that mean this "shortcut" won't work for you?

Not at all. Because I guarantee you *still* have a problem with your tongue. Controlling your speech isn't just about anger management. There's a lot more to it. For instance …

Do you ever lie?

Do you ever brag?

Do you ever complain?

Do you ever gossip?

Do you ever ridicule others?

Do you ever rashly judge people?

Do you ever blabber on endlessly?

Do you ever use silent body language to convey your anger or sarcastic "tones" of voice?

Come on, be honest! You know you do. We *all* do.

Guarding our speech and controlling our tongues isn't just about the nasty things we say. It's about all the garbage that comes out of our mouths on a daily basis. Christ was very clear about the matter. He told His disciples, "When you have to say yes, say yes; when you have to say no, say no. Anything else is from the evil one" (see Matt. 5:37). What could be simpler to understand?

I'm not claiming it's easy to be perfect in your speech. It's not. Shortcuts can be difficult—brutally difficult. But that's why this one works. Christ said at another time that what "defiles" a person is not what goes into his body but rather, what "comes out of his mouth"—because what comes out of the mouth really originates in the heart (Matt. 15:11). That's the true source of all our pride and greed and jealousy and lust and gluttony and laziness and anger.

Therefore, if we somehow manage to stop the outpouring of filth, we're bound to see a change in our lives. If we have the kind of strength it takes to control the exit point of all our verbal toxins, we're going to be victorious over all our other sins as well—including the secret ones we never utter a word about. That's why St. James said, "Any man among you who is perfect in speech is a perfect man."

So, yes, it's going to be hard. But luckily this book isn't about instantaneous success. It's about building momentum. It's about getting on the right road to peace and happiness and staying there. As with everything else we've talked about, we're going to move forward a little bit at a time.

With that in mind, if you're the type of person who curses frequently, then for the next few days, you should try to eliminate all expletives from your speech. No more obscenities. No more vulgarities. No more excuses. Just stop cold.

If you're the type of person who doesn't have a problem with profanity, then try something else. Pick two or three of the other imperfections listed above and eliminate those from your speech. For example, stop bragging! There's no need to talk about all the good things you've accomplished. There's no need to even tell your side of the story every time you have a disagreement with someone. God already knows your side of the story. God already knows your accomplishments. *He's* the one you should be trying to impress.

If you don't have a bragging problem, then stop gossiping for once in your life! Or stop complaining!

In fact, you might want to try cutting down on your talking, period. Try being more silent for a change. Remember, Christ lived thirty years in silence before He started His public ministry, and even then, during the busiest, most hectic parts of that ministry, He always took time to withdraw in silence so He could speak and listen to His Father in Heaven. That's the way He prepared Himself for even more profound activity.

St. Francis of Assisi said that we should preach the gospel always—with words, if necessary. We have to get it through our heads that silence is not something negative. It's not simply an "absence" of noise. In fact, it's the opposite. It's a positive action we can take to combat the distracting and destructive power of noise in our lives. Silence is sacred. Silence is mystical. Silence allows our bodies and our spirits to breathe. It helps to lead us to inward reflection and contemplation. In fact, silence almost always results in greater intimacy with God because it's in silence that God speaks to us most clearly. You can bet your last dollar that if someone is an insufferable chatterbox, that person is usually very far from making any truly deep decisions that will change his or her life for the better. So in addition to controlling your tongue in the other ways I mentioned, take my advice and just *shhh*!

Try to do your best to discipline your tongue—at least for the remainder of the time it takes to finish this book. And then, if you like the transformation that occurs, by all means continue the process. Ultimately, the goal here isn't just to clean up your speech. It's to clean up your soul. If you tame your tongue, you tame yourself. If you conquer your mouth, you conquer your life.

And if you experience any setbacks along the way—as you certainly will—just keep reminding yourself of the importance of perspective. Keep thinking of those ancient mystics and their wise old sayings:

Quid hoc ad aeternitatem?—What is this in light of eternity?

Memento mori!—Remember you will die!

Action Items

✓ Make a list of all your imperfections of speech. Pick two or three, and for the remainder of this month, ruthlessly eliminate them from your life. If you find yourself indulging in one of those imperfections out of habit, pause, calmly recollect yourself, and do an about-face.

Rest, Review, Celebrate

Congratulations! You've made it through two weeks. You're already halfway through this program. That's great! If you fasted yesterday, then enjoy a wonderful meal today. If you didn't, then make sure you fast next week sometime. Take a few minutes today to review your notes. Have you done all your action items? If not, go back and do them right now! If you have done them, how do you feel? Take today to rest and celebrate your accomplishments. Go to church and continue to thank God for the help He is giving you to turn your life around.

See you tomorrow!

WEEK THREE

Put Your Priorities in Order

Time to Get Off the Fence

Hopefully you've been building some momentum and laying the groundwork for what might become an important transformation in your life. If you have, that's great. I would love to shake your hand because you're already way ahead of most people in this world. But now we're about to enter a new phase. We've come to a point where we really need to make a few decisions.

Every decision you make in life—even the smallest—has the potential to be important because every decision starts you down a pathway. Take an example from aviation. You know that a jet can depart from New York and fly toward Rome, but if it changes course as much as a few degrees at the beginning, its flight path will be altered by hundreds of miles. By the time the plane gets across the ocean, it will be headed to a completely different city—maybe even a completely different continent.

That's the way it is in life sometimes. It's possible for you to make a very quiet decision—a decision no one else knows about—that changes everything. It might take years for the difference to become noticeable. But in reality, the whole flight path of your existence has been altered.

That has happened to me a couple of times. I remember once when I was in my mid-twenties, I was sitting down at the family table having lunch. It was just a normal summer Sunday, and I was munching on a sandwich and reading the newspaper. The TV was on in the background, and my mother and father and brothers were all hanging around, talking. Suddenly my younger sister walked through the door and casually threw on the table a plastic bag that contained a few metal crosses on chains. She said that someone she knew at church had given them to her and that if I wanted, I could take one.

Now, at the time, I wasn't a serious Catholic at all. I never prayed or went to church or read the Bible or tried to obey any of the commandments. In fact, I couldn't have named the commandments if you asked me. Sure, there had been times when I thought about God and wondered whether I really believed in Him; and of course at Christmas and Easter I occasionally attended Mass. But all I was really interested in were girls. God was absolutely nowhere on my radar screen. And yet, for some unknown reason, on that lazy, ordinary summer afternoon, I found myself staring at that bag of crosses.

I had never liked wearing jewelry, but I decided I would try one on—just to see what it was like. After all, I spent a lot of time going to the beach, and it might look "cool" to wear something around my neck. So I found the plainest cross in the bag—one that wasn't fancy or expensive at all, just simple stainless steel—and put it on.

And then something interesting happened. Just at the moment I clasped the chain around my neck, a very quiet but very clear thought occurred to me: *Does this mean I'm a Christian?*

At that point in my life, I knew very little about Christianity. I certainly didn't have any kind of relationship with Christ. So I asked myself: Do I want to just wear this cross for no reason—or do I perhaps want to find out more about what it means? Without really thinking, I made a decision. I would keep the cross on for a little while to see if I liked it, and at the same time I would try to pick up a book during the week to at least refresh myself on the basics of Catholicism.

All of this happened in my mind very quickly. The newspaper and half-eaten sandwich were still in front of me. The TV was on, and my family was talking in the background. I went right back to eating lunch. On the surface, it seemed as if nothing had happened. And yet something monumental had happened. A *sacramental* of the Church—a little cross—had acted as a channel of God's grace into my soul. With the help of that grace, I made a decision that put me on a very specific path, a path that would lead me—over the course of several decades—on a great adventure, an adventure that has ultimately culminated in your reading these words right now.

Do you see what I'm trying to get at? The power of decisions can never be underestimated. Even the tiniest ones can change your life forever. That's why we need to start discussing them now. In fact, there are three in particular we need to focus on. And the first of these is the most critical.

We've talked a little in this book about God. But now it's time to get serious about Him. Now it's time to make a genuine decision about faith.

So many people mistakenly think that faith is a feeling. It's not. It's a decision. Feelings are mushy. Feelings are inconsistent. Feelings are *deceptive*.

For example, did you know that right now you're speeding through the galaxy at 67,000 miles per hour? That's how fast the earth is traveling around the sun. But do you *feel* that you're moving? Or do you feel stationary?

And what about your body? Do you know that you're actually made up of 6.5 *octillion* atoms—that's a billion billion billion—all of them separate from one another? But do you *feel* as if you're broken into all those pieces? Of course not.

And that's why you can't always trust your feelings. They're unreliable.

Moreover, feelings go up and down too much. One day you feel depressed; the next day you feel elated. One moment you feel that everything is black and cloudy. The next moment you feel a glimmer of hope, and everything is sunshine. Sometimes what you eat makes you feel a certain way. Sometimes the weather makes you feel a certain way. Sometimes the music you hear makes you feel a certain way. Sometimes a particular person or place or occasion makes you feel a certain way. Sometimes you know why you feel the way you do; sometimes you have no clue. Feelings can be joyous or exhilarating or passionate or hateful or dull or depressing—but the one thing they never seem to be is predictable.

Personal-development experts love to talk about the ability we have to change our feelings; to do things that make us feel confident, motivated, empowered, and so forth. And they're right. We *can* change them. We're *not* slaves to them. But it takes work to alter our emotions—hard work. There's a certain moral and emotional "gravity" that's always trying to pull us down, trying to keep us from being on an even keel. In fact, there's a theological reason for this that goes back to the Garden of Eden and our fallen human nature. We'll talk more about that later. But the point is that no matter how successful we are at controlling our feelings, we're always going to be on an emotional roller coaster to some extent. And we just can't afford to base the most important decisions of our lives on what amounts to a ride.

Now let's tie this into the subject of faith by using a couple of other practical examples. Most human bodies, because of their specific gravity and other physiological traits, have a natural tendency to float on the water and to rise to the surface if submerged. Even when a person is not particularly buoyant, it doesn't take much physical effort to stay above water. That's a scientific fact. We can give that fact the full assent of our intellect and know that it's true, but when learning how to swim, we don't necessarily *feel* it to be true. The same can be said when it comes to flying in a plane. It's a fact that air molecules moving over the curved surface of a wing at a certain speed will result in aerodynamic lift. We can give that principle of physics the full assent of our intellect. But that doesn't mean we don't sometimes have trouble *feeling* confident that a four-hundred-ton jumbo jet can fly off the ground and cruise safely at thirty-five thousand feet in the air. In both these cases, our feelings and our knowledge of the truth might not align. And in both these cases, the best way to cultivate a feeling of certitude is to act on the basis of our intellectual knowledge. In other words, it's only after acting on a *decision of the will* that we are often able to gain true emotional "faith" in the safety of swimming or flying.

It's the same with our faith in God.

Let's be honest. Sometimes it's easy to *feel* that God exists and that He loves us. Other times—especially when someone we love dies—it's easy to feel that He's silent or nonexistent. I've got news for you: even if you were the holiest person in the world and had the most fervent faith, there still might be times when you'd feel like an agnostic or even an atheist. Does that surprise you? It shouldn't. Some of the most famous saints in history (St. Teresa of Calcutta, for instance) have gone through periods of profound spiritual darkness, periods when they didn't have any strong emotional feelings about God, when they felt totally "dry." Did that prevent them from being holy? Did it prevent them from having faith? Not a bit. Their feelings may have wavered, but their faith never did. I can't emphasize this enough: the world of faith and the world of feelings are two entirely different things, and sometimes they exist on two entirely different planes.

Even if you were to witness a bona fide miracle, it still wouldn't "prove" that God exists. God Himself has told us this. He has made it abundantly clear that faith is a *test*—not a demonstration. And if you've spent any time at all in school, you know that while a test is in progress, the teacher is usually silent. So if you're waiting around to see some great blazing cross appear in the sky, you're going to be waiting a long time. God just isn't going to show Himself to us in bodily form. He isn't going to materialize and start performing miracles and raising people from the dead. He did that once before and got crucified for it! No. The next time He comes back will be the end of the world.

God has said time and again that we have to believe in Him *without* the benefit of seeing with our eyes. He has given us all the information we need—all the evidence of nature and logic and common sense and reliable testimonies and revelation—but He's left it to us to make the final decision, despite how our feelings might fluctuate.

And don't think that atheists have any kind of free pass when it comes to emotional highs and lows either. They don't. If you've been struggling with faith, your doubts aren't going to magically disappear if you decide to bite the bullet and become an unbeliever. There are still going to be moments when you have the feeling that God *does* exist. There will still be quiet, eerie nights when you gaze up at the vast array of stars sparkling in the heavens and feel deep down that there *has to be* some Being who created it all. There will still be times when you hear a powerful piece of music or see a beautiful painting or read a deeply moving passage of literature, and your soul stirs inside you and whispers that there *must* be some grand cosmic Artist behind it all. There will still be moments when you're in the midst of great suffering, and out of nowhere, a friend or a stranger does something so kind, so compassionate, so *good*, that you actually break down in tears and feel that there must be such a thing as the human *spirit*—a spirit made in the image and likeness of Goodness itself.

The bottom line is that the atheist position is just too full of holes for anyone to really feel certain about it. I've discussed this before in other books, but it's worth repeating now. Atheists are always claiming that it's "superstitious" to believe in God. But the exact opposite is true. There are dozens of logical arguments for God's existence. It's atheism that's founded on a superstition—a superstition that says that life has no meaning.

We *know* life has meaning—it's preposterous to deny it. Just think about it for a moment. Atheists want us to believe that the world is made up of *physical objects* and nothing else. They want us to believe that everything in life—our thoughts, our dreams, our passions, our loves, our hates, our hopes, our joys, our virtues, our sins, our griefs, our guilt, our philosophies, our arts, our politics, our literature, our music, our history, our deepest desire for God and love and perfect happiness and eternal life, all that is transcendent in the world, all that is good and true and beautiful—that *everything* is purely the result of biochemical reactions and the random movement of lifeless atoms in an empty and lifeless ether and that life is nothing but a freak, cosmic accident, devoid of any plan or purpose!

That's not logic. That's not science. That's faith! What's more, it's an irrational, unwarranted, and gullible faith that serves as the foundation for all superstition.

But there's even more. Atheists make a whole slew of assumptions that can't be proven scientifically. For instance, they believe that this incredibly complex universe of ours—a universe of unparalleled beauty, harmony, and order—came about all by itself, out of nothing. They believe that order came out of chaos, that life came out of lifelessness, that consciousness came out of nonconsciousness, that reason came out of irrationality.

None of these beliefs can be proven empirically. None can be demonstrated or replicated scientifically. None of them even makes sense.

And that's why the truly great scientists in history have never been stone-cold atheists. In fact, most of them have fervently believed in God.

Aristotle, Francis Bacon, Leonardo da Vinci, and Isaac Newton all believed in God. The father of chemistry, Antoine Lavoisier, believed in God. The father of rocket science, Wernher von Braun, believed in God. The first person to artificially split the atom, Ernest Walton, believed in God. The Belgian astronomer who proposed the big bang theory of the origin of the universe, Georges Lemaître, not only believed in God but was a Roman Catholic priest! The father of genetics—the science that provides the basis for the whole theory of evolution—was Gregor Mendel, an Augustinian monk!

Even Albert Einstein, who did not subscribe to the tenets of any religion, recoiled when people erroneously said that he didn't believe in God: "I am not an atheist!" he stated emphatically. "In the view of such harmony in the cosmos which I, with my limited human mind, am able to recognize, there are yet people who say there is no God. But what really makes me angry is that they quote me for the support of such views."[3]

[3] Ronald W. Clark, *Einstein: The Life and Times* (New York: World Publishing, 1971), 425.

Einstein knew there was something more to the universe than he or anyone else could understand. In fact, he once said: "The most beautiful emotion we can experience is the mystical. It is the sower of all true art and science. He to whom this emotion is a stranger, who can no longer wonder and stand rapt in awe, is as good as dead."[4]

As good as dead, he said!

Is that what you want to be—as good as dead?

And bear in mind, these are just a few of the world's scientists. We haven't even mentioned the greatest historians, painters, sculptors, architects, musicians, novelists, poets, generals, monarchs, explorers, and doctors. If we did, you could bet every last dollar you have that the overwhelming majority believed in God. Why?

It's simple. All of these great geniuses knew there had to be something else in life besides physical matter. They all recognized the fact that the deeper you go into the sciences, the more mysterious the universe is.

There's simply no scientific answer to the question "Where did everything come from?" There's no scientific answer to the question "How can matter be eternal?" There's no scientific answer to the question "How can something come from nothing?" There's no scientific answer to the question "Why is the universe so organized?" There's no scientific answer to the question "How did life arise from lifelessness?"

Scientists don't have the answer to any of these questions, and they never will. So if you think atheism is the solution to your doubts, you've been misinformed.

[4] David Rowe and Robert Schulmann, *Einstein on Politics: His Private Thoughts and Public Stands on Nationalism, Zionism, War, Peace, and the Bomb* (Princeton: Princeton University Press, 2007), 229.

That road leads only to more uncertainties and more riddles. The fact is that nothing you do or read is ever going to give you anything resembling a mathematical proof either that God exists or that He doesn't exist. It always comes back to the necessity of making a choice. You must make a choice.

And I mean *must*. That's the point so many people miss. They think they can just sail through life without making a real decision about God and it won't cost them anything. What self-delusion! We've been so brainwashed into believing that the greatest thing in the world to have is an "open mind" and that the greatest thing to do is "search" for answers. But that's nonsense. The whole point of searching for something is to eventually find it. The whole point of having an open mind is so that it can eventually close—on the truth! An open mind is not an amorphous mind. A worthwhile search is not an endless, hopeless one. Don't believe the lies of the world. If you're past twenty-five and haven't made a definitive decision about God, then you've got your priorities misaligned. You can't afford to waste any more of your life. It's time to get off the fence!

Look, making a decision doesn't involve just assessing all the facts. It involves assessing all the *risks*. And there are huge risks associated with rejecting God. You may not be aware of them because the world never talks about them.

But the fact is, you're called to a *greatness* the world knows nothing about. You're called to a *peace* the world knows nothing about. You're called to a *love* the world knows nothing about. You're called to a supernatural end—*Heaven*—the world knows nothing about. All those things result from having a relationship with God. When you cut God off, you cut them off too.

Let's say I gave you a key to an old storage unit I owned and said you could keep whatever was inside—maybe some pieces of furniture worth a few hundred dollars. You might take the key, or you might not, depending on your situation. But what if I were some eccentric old billionaire and gave you a key to my personal bank vault? What if I told you that I wasn't quite sure, but there *might* be a cash box there with at least a million dollars inside? Would you take the key from me then? I bet you would. I bet you wouldn't be able to grab it from my hands fast enough. And it wouldn't matter one bit whether you were sure there was money inside—the *possibility* would just be too great to pass by.

Or let's come at it from the opposite angle. Let's say you notice a stray wire coming out of some battery-operated device in your kitchen. It wouldn't be any big deal if you touched it, right? Even if the device were turned on, the electric current just wouldn't be that strong. The most you'd get from touching it would be a little shock. But what if a twenty-thousand-volt cable were placed in front of you? Would you take the chance of grabbing hold of that? Would it matter much if you didn't know if the electricity was on or off? Of course not! You'd be crazy to take *any* kind of chance with it.

Are you getting what I'm saying here? When it comes to deciding whether or not to have faith, the risk-reward ratio is all in God's favor. That's not meant to scare you. It's just the plain truth. If you choose to deny God, you stand to lose everything. If you choose to believe in Him, you stand to gain everything.

It's up to you to decide which it's going to be. And it doesn't matter one bit how you feel. Remember the story in the Gospels about the man who begged Jesus to heal his son? The boy had been suffering from some kind of demonic illness since childhood, and no one could cure him. But Jesus assured him, "If you believe, all things are possible." To which the father responded: "Lord, I believe; Help my unbelief!" (see Mark 9:23–24).

That really captures everything I've been trying to say here. Without hesitating, the father declared his *decision*: "I believe."

But he followed it up immediately with an emotional plea: "Help my unbelief." What he was basically saying was that despite his free-will choice, there was still a part of him that didn't *feel* faith.

But what did Jesus do? Did He criticize the man? Did He tell him he had to have more faith? No! He immediately reached out and healed the man's son. In other words, the man's decision to believe was enough. It was all Christ required to grant his request and show him the healing power of God.

The same goes for you and me. I said before that even if you decide to believe, your feelings might sometimes waver—especially during periods of grief or tragedy. But I wasn't quite giving you the whole story. I didn't say that after you make your faith decision, something else will happen too. In the deepest part of your being—the part made in the image and likeness of God—a different kind of certitude will begin to form. Only this certitude will be based not on feelings but on grace—a gift of divine help from God Himself. And once this faith takes hold, it will grow and grow and grow until it literally transforms every aspect of your life. It will take away your fear. It will take away your loneliness. It will take away your despair. It will give you an entirely new perspective—a perspective that transcends all emotions and all feelings and all circumstances. You see, when you get to know God, instead of just knowing *about* Him, everything changes.

So stop worrying about whether you have enough faith! Of course you do! God gives *everyone* the gift of faith (see 2 Pet. 3:9). But the gift has to be unwrapped! It has to be opened! And the way you open it is by choosing to believe regardless of how you might feel.

Why not make that choice now? Why not decide once and for all that there *is* a God? And then act that way. Live your life as someone who believes.

How do you do that? I'm glad you asked. Read on!

Action Items

- ✓ If you're an atheist or an agnostic, read this chapter over again and think about it very carefully. Even if you don't feel that you're ready to believe in God, make a decision to believe in Him at least for the remainder of this month. You can change that decision at any time. But for now, write down these words: I, [your name], make a decision today, [date], to believe in God.
- ✓ If you're already a believing Christian or a practicing Catholic, find the Apostles' Creed online and copy it out in your notebook or paste it in your computer document. Then pray it slowly, thinking about each article of faith, and giving it the full, conscious assent of your will. Don't worry about any emotional doubts you might have about the specific tenets of Christianity. Just assert your decision to believe. After you're finished, write or type your name and the date below it.

Getting Straight with God

So now we come to the hard part.

Maybe you think we've already talked about some difficult things. I disagree. Up till now, we really haven't had to make any *sacrifices*. Even deciding to have faith doesn't cost us anything—at least not in the beginning. But now it's time to start putting together some of these random ideas we've been discussing. And whenever you put something together—especially something magnificent, like your life—you always have to leave something out. It's the leaving-out part that hurts.

In this case, we have to start ruthlessly eliminating some of our pride. Pride is the main reason people aren't sorry for the sins they commit—and that's what we're going to focus on now: being sorry for sins.

Notice I said *sins*. Not faults, not weaknesses, not shortcomings, not any of those words the world uses to make us feel better about ourselves. The world is always trying to confuse us when it comes to this subject. It's always trying to make us ignore the reality of who we are, how we act, and what we do wrong. Well, it's time to get unconfused.

Sinning is the act of offending God. It's doing things that are wrong in *God's* eyes, not necessarily *our* eyes. And that's why people's screens go up so fast whenever we broach this subject. Nobody ever wants to be told that they're doing something wrong. We spoke a little on Day 3 about our secret selves—all the toxic thoughts and desires we keep buried inside and never tell anyone about because we *know* how horrible they are. But what happens the moment someone else tries to point those facts out? How defensive do we get? How defensive do *you* get?

That's when all the comparisons start flying, isn't it? There's such a thing as "comparison morality." It's when we say things like "Yes, it's true that I've cheated on my spouse, but *compared with* all the other nice things I do, I'm really not so terrible. After all, I'm kind and generous, and I always try to help people, so the balance doesn't come out too bad."

The balance! As if life were some kind of financial ledger and our only task were to tabulate our assets and liabilities and make sure the bottom line came out a credit.

We're so muddled in our thinking. Even if what we've done wrong makes up only a fraction of the overall good we've accomplished, that still doesn't make the wrong things *less wrong*. We've got to stop patting ourselves on the back so much. We all do a lot of good things—and we all do a lot of bad things. The ratio isn't the important thing.

Or sometimes we say, "Hey, I'm not a criminal. Just read the newspaper and look at all those thugs out there—all the thieves and rapists and murderers. I don't do any of that. *Compared with them*, I'm a good person."

See? There we go again! We're so busy looking at other people! We just can't help ourselves. We're always spinning our heads in this direction or that, trying to observe the sins of others. And then we wonder why we get so dizzy and confused. The truth is, there's only one place to look: up, at God. And there's only one question to ask Him: "How have I failed You?"

It doesn't matter if we think we're good people. So what if we're good? Congratulations to us! It's wonderful that we've managed to avoid a life of crime. But the morally relevant question to ask is not "How do my sins compare with other people's sins?" It's "What are *my* sins?" That's the only thing that ultimately matters in terms of our peace and happiness.

And this is where the world really works against our happiness. The world is always saying that our problems aren't due to sins at all but rather to the "guilt" we feel—all that nasty guilt caused by "religion." I'm sure you've heard this before. There's "Christian guilt" and "Catholic guilt" and "Irish guilt" and "Italian guilt" and every other kind of guilt imaginable. According to the world, all of it is unhealthy and psychologically damaging. According to the world, life would be so wonderful if there were no such thing as guilt.

But do you know the truth? That's a lot of baloney! It's impossible to live in a world without guilt. Anytime you have a code of conduct, there's going to be some kind of guilt associated with it—and it doesn't matter what that code is. To be in a family means that you have to follow a certain code of conduct. To be in a friendship means that you have to follow a certain code of conduct. To be at a job means that you have to follow a certain code of conduct. To be in a romantic relationship means that you have to follow a certain code of conduct.

And guess what? If you fail to live up to the code of conduct you're supposed to follow, you're going to experience some form of guilt. Whenever you have rules of *any* kind, there are bound to be people who feel guilty when they *break* those rules. That's just common sense.

Do you think Hollywood, for instance, has its own "moral" code of conduct—its own belief system about what's right and wrong, what's sacred and what's okay to attack or lampoon? You bet your life it does! And if you work in the movie business and you violate that code (for example, if you attend a pro-life rally), you can be sure there are going to be serious repercussions for your career—*unless* (maybe) you express a certain amount of guilt and contrition.

The point is that when the world voices its "concern" about Christian guilt, it doesn't object one bit to the guilt itself. Let's stop being naïve! What it objects to is the code of conduct—the Christian code of conduct. It objects to the Ten Commandments, the moral teachings of Christ in the Gospels, the moral teachings proclaimed by the Christian Church for the last two thousand years. *That's* what the world despises.

What the world doesn't realize, of course, is that the Christian code isn't just some collection of man-made rules and regulations designed to make us feel bad. It's the way God meant us to live. It's the code that God Himself created, and it's one that has been written into the hearts of every man and woman on the planet. So when we violate it, there are bound to be feelings of guilt, at least on some level.

This whole question really comes back to the reality of sin and what it does to us. We mentioned earlier that sinning causes a kind of spiritual chaos in our souls—a disintegration, a division. It actually separates us on three levels. First, it separates us from ourselves—from who we truly are in God's eyes. Second, it separates us from other people, causing friction and sometimes even havoc in our personal relationships. Finally, it separates us from God, who is the very opposite of sin.

Every single time we sin, these three divisions take place—and this affects us. Christ said that a house divided against itself cannot stand (Mark 3:25). So what do you think happens when we keep chopping ourselves up in this fashion over a long period of time? We collapse. We crumble. We implode. No one has to tell us to feel unhappy. No one has to tell us to feel guilty. It happens all on its own—because it's built into our very nature.

Now, what we do with those guilty feelings is up to us. And this is where we have a few critical decisions to make—because the guilt we feel can be either destructive or fruitful.

Some people try to ignore their guilt and learn to live with it. After all, you can learn to live with practically anything in life, can't you? But it's hard. The guilt is always there, right under the surface, eating away at you. And many times you might not even know the reason. It's almost like having termites in your house. They can infest the wood structure for years without ever being discovered. You can put all kinds of money into remodeling the exterior of your home and making everything beautiful on the outside. But meanwhile, beneath the glittering façade, the whole thing is coming to pieces.

That's exactly what some people do to themselves. They make lots of money and achieve lots of success in the eyes of the world, and they're still not happy. Then they go to psychologists or take personal-development courses, and they sometimes seem to make progress—for a while—but once the emotional high wears off, they're no happier than they were before. And the reason is that they haven't addressed the root problem—*not their guilt* but their sins.

Then there are people who *do* realize they've done something morally wrong and regret it. But the regret they feel is a very *human* kind. They regret that they did something that got them into trouble. They regret that they got caught. They essentially feel stupid and frustrated and angry at themselves.

Whenever people experience this kind of regret, they always have a tendency to focus inwardly and dwell on the sins they committed. Have you ever done that? Have you ever played your sins over and over again in your head like a broken record, until you've worked yourself up into a kind of hopeless remorse? There's really no way out of that kind of thinking. It's an infinite loop of frustration and self-recrimination. Many people go through life that way. They're just content to stew in their own guilt, to lie there feeling helpless in a puddle of mud without making any real effort to get out.

Finally, there are people who take a different approach—a sensible approach. These folks know they've done something wrong and regret it, but instead of focusing inward on their own guilt and sins, they go *outside* themselves—to God. Instead of letting their regret turn into hopeless despair, they lift their heads up to Heaven and say, "Lord, I'm sorry. Please forgive me." In other words, they make a *decision*—based on their faith in God and their hope in His mercy—to explicitly confess their sins and ask for forgiveness.

And guess what? God forgives them. Every single time.

You see, once you get over your pride, being forgiven for your sins is actually the easiest thing in the world. God *wants* to make it easy for you. He wants to have mercy on you. He wants to help you move quickly from regret to reconciliation. He knows that once reconciliation takes place, healing can finally begin.

Healing, as we all know, is very different from forgiveness. Forgiveness is an event, something God does for you at a specific moment, when you ask Him for it and when you're correctly disposed to it. Healing, on the other hand, is a *process*—sometimes a long and difficult process. But it's a process that's necessary.

Here's an easy way to understand it. If you take a hammer and drive a nail into the wall, you can remove the nail, but there will still be a hole there, right? Likewise, if you've been forgiven for a sin, there will still be an open wound that remains. Sometimes the wound is leftover emotional pain. Sometimes it's a broken relationship. Sometimes it's the need for some kind of reparation or restitution. Whatever it is, the wound has to be healed, just as the hole from the nail has to be filled. It's the same principle.

The good news is that once God forgives you, He also gives you all the grace you require to go through the healing process—all the humility, all the peace, all the patience, all the perseverance, all the hope, all the wisdom, all the love that you need. It's in receiving all these *other* spiritual graces that you can grow as a human being and experience greater peace and happiness.

Unlike human regret, true reconciliation always leads to happiness because it always leads to greater union with God, and as we've said before in this book, union with God is the key to everything in life. Therefore, if you've made the decision to have faith, the next decision should be simple. You should decide *right now* to give Him your sins too—every single one.

No matter where you are in your spiritual life, the moment you've finished reading these words, you should put this book down and make a real effort to think about your sins. Then, without any fuss, you should immediately ask God for forgiveness. And you should make a decision to go on asking for forgiveness whenever you fall and no matter how many times you fall.

Now, if you're a Catholic, you have an added obligation of going to Confession—of making use of what's called the sacrament of Reconciliation.

Catholics believe that Christ Himself instituted this sacrament when He lived and walked in Palestine two thousand years ago. At that time, after He breathed on the apostles—a sign that He was giving them the Holy Spirit—He said to them: "If you forgive the sins of any, they are forgiven; if you retain the sins of any, they are retained" (John 20:23). Later on, St. Paul confirmed this authority to forgive sins, when he said: "All this is from God, who through Christ reconciled us to himself and gave us the ministry of reconciliation" (2 Cor. 5:18).

It would take too much time and space to go over the theology of this sacrament now, but suffice to say that the Church is charged with a special "ministry of reconciliation." And believe me, it is one of the most wonderful things about being a Catholic. Oftentimes, Protestants feel compelled to give their "testimony" before large groups of worshippers, confessing their sins to everyone. That's not something a Catholic is ever expected to do. Rather, we confess our sins in a small room, anonymously, to a validly ordained priest who can't see us and who is sworn to secrecy. Moreover, we believe that that priest—though undoubtedly as sinful as any other human being—has the authority to stand *in persona Christi*, a Latin phrase that means "in the person of Christ." In other words, we don't believe that another person is forgiving us. We believe that when the priest says the sacred words "I absolve you from your sins in the name of the Father, and of the Son, and of the Holy Spirit," it is not he who is bestowing forgiveness but rather Jesus Christ. At the moment of absolution, Christ is mystically and sacramentally present—just as He was when He forgave sins during biblical times. That's why the priest says "*I* absolve you" and not "Christ absolves you."

Some Catholics still object to this. They don't care that the priest is standing in the person of Christ. They don't care that God wants sinners to make use of the sacrament of Reconciliation that He instituted. "No, no, no," they say, "I'm not telling my sins to any man."

I have to laugh when I hear Catholics speak this way. I think to myself: Really? So you don't want to tell your sins to someone else? Well, you don't seem to have a problem telling *other* people's sins to everyone around you! You don't seem to have a problem gossiping whenever the mood strikes you. You don't seem to have a problem telling your best friend or your next-door neighbor or your hairdresser or your golfing buddy or your bartender or anyone within a fifty-mile radius all the sins and secrets and intimate details you happen to know about your own family, friends, and acquaintances. Yet when God asks you to confess *your* sins to one of His specially designated ministers, *then* you have a problem; *then* you suddenly get offended and tight-lipped.

Please! Let's not be so naïve!

These Catholics aren't fooling anyone by pretending to be innocent—least of all, God. We've got to stop lying to ourselves. We've got to be more humble. We've got to admit that when it comes to having our sins forgiven, we don't know more than God does. God understands human psychology better than we do because He *created* it. He knows how comforting it is for us to be *sure* that we've been forgiven for our sins. That's one of the main reasons Christ instituted the sacrament of Reconciliation—because of the certitude it can give us that we're free to make a clean start. God knows that those beautiful words we hear the priest say at the end of Confession—"Your sins have been forgiven; go in peace"—have the added psychological benefit of making the healing process much quicker and easier.

I know I sound like some preacher now, but no matter what religion you practice, there's really nothing more important that all of us can do than ask God for forgiveness. I say "all of us" because we're all sinners. We've all got to stop this nonsense of blaming other people for our guilt. We've all got to stop letting our pride get in the way of our relationship with God. We've all got to relinquish ourselves. We've all got to wipe the slate clean—to completely surrender. It doesn't matter how many times we've committed a particular sin. Once it has been forgiven, it's gone forever—along with all the other sins, offenses, obscenities, evils, and bad behavior of our past life—all of it gone and forgotten; dead and crucified.

That's right—gone forever. That's the teaching of Christianity. The Bible makes the solemn promise that once God forgives us, He "casts all our sins into the depths of the ocean" (see Micah 7:19). And to that line, various spiritual writers have added: "Then God places a sign there that says *No fishing allowed!*"

Action Items

- ✓ Make a list of all your major sins. Use abbreviations or code words if you're worried that someone may gain access to the list. Tell God you're sorry for each sin and ask for His forgiveness. Moreover, tell Him you're going to try as hard as you can not to commit those sins again.
- ✓ If you're a Catholic, go online and check the parish bulletins of some local churches. Many churches offer the sacrament of Reconciliation on Saturdays. Some churches offer it more often. In most cases, you can call your local parish and schedule a Confession for any day of the week. Make a decision *today* about when you're going to Confession. Then put it on your calendar. The sooner, the better. Before you go, check online to refresh your memory about how to make a good Confession. Finally, if you don't already know the Act of Contrition, find it online and print it out so you can repeat it in the confessional before the priest gives you absolution.

Free as a Bird

Let's take a moment to recap the last two chapters. We've been discussing spiritual decisions: specifically, the decision to have faith and the decision to repent of our sins. We're going to add a third one now: the decision to forgive people when they sin against us. These three decisions really make up one piece.

Some people don't understand that. They think that *all* you need to get to Heaven is faith in God. And in a sense, that's true. But it really depends on what you mean by "faith." Faith *isn't* just believing in God. After all, the devil believes in God, doesn't he? And so do all the demons. And so do many, many evil people right here on earth. They believe in Him, but they hate Him. Did you ever realize that?

Belief is just one part of the faith equation. Real faith involves not just accepting God's existence but turning *to* God and away from sin. It's an attempt to be in ever-greater union with God. It's an embrace of godliness. And in order to do that, you have to be sorry when you sin, and you have to forgive others when they sin against you. There are really three separate components to the one faith decision.

If you like, you can think of faith as a bird. The body of the bird is our belief in God's existence. But a bird also has two wings—and those wings are repentance and forgiveness.

Now, can a bird fly without its wings? Or can it fly with just one of its wings? Of course not. In order for a bird to get off the ground and fly up to the sky, it has got to use both wings—and not just once but all the time. It has to keep flapping its wings, over and over again. When it stops using both wings, it stops flying. The same is true for us. When we stop repenting of our sins and when we stop forgiving others, we stop flying. And not only that, but we crash to the ground.

Let's talk for a moment about this second "wing"—forgiving others. A very experienced Christian counselor once told me that he thought that 80 to 90 percent of the problems people face are the result of their unwillingness to forgive others. The reason he believed that—and why I agree with him—is that when you withhold your forgiveness, you very nearly cut yourself off from God's grace and make it extremely difficult for Him to help you with all the other challenges you have in life, whether they're emotional, relational, marital, financial, or psychological in nature. Cutting yourself off from God's grace is like cutting the anchor line from your boat when you're in the middle of a stormy sea. It's dumb. Even worse, it's dangerous. And that's why you really have to think twice before you withhold your forgiveness from anyone.

There's an awful lot of confusion surrounding the topic of forgiveness. Many people have a mistaken notion of what it means to forgive someone and what it doesn't mean. Forgiveness does *not* mean that you give up your right to self-defense. Everyone has the right to protect themselves from harm, from abuse, from lies, from slander. If you're in some kind of abusive relationship, God doesn't expect you to stay in it. He expects you to change it or leave it. Never forget that you have an immortal soul and are made in the image and likeness of God. You have more value than all the stars and planets in the universe put together. You should *never* be a doormat or a punching bag for anyone.

Forgiveness also doesn't have anything to do with good feelings. As I've said before, it's impossible for human beings to have full control over their emotions. If someone hurts you badly, God doesn't expect you to feel all warm and fuzzy toward that person. Nor do you have to respect what that person did. When someone does something wicked, it deserves condemnation. Forgiving someone doesn't ever mean calling evil good. That's a lie. And the father of lies is the devil—not God. God *never* lies.

The fact is that forgiveness doesn't reside in the emotions at all but rather in the *will*. If you had to calmly decide the destiny of the person who harmed you, what choice would you make? That's the kind of thing God is interested in knowing. It's perfectly okay to want bad people to be brought to justice on earth if they've done something wrong or criminal. But what you can't ever do is wish *evil* upon them. You can't hope that they get a disease or go to Hell. That's up to God—not you.

Forgiveness basically means that even if you have negative feelings toward certain people, you still wish them well; in fact, you still wish them the greatest possible good, which is Heaven. It means that even if you're revolted by the thought of those people, and even if you've legitimately chosen never to associate with them again, you still hope that they embrace God, that they're sorry for their sins, and that they ultimately receive salvation. Christ spelled it out very clearly when He said that we have to "love our enemies and pray for those who persecute us" (see Matt. 5:44). Praying is really the acid test when it comes to forgiveness. It's the bare minimum we have to do for those who have hurt us.

Now, how do you pray for people who have hurt you—maybe even hurt you badly or abused you?

In some cases, it can be extraordinarily difficult. In fact, sometimes the best and easiest thing to do is simply to pray that God deals with those people in His own way; in whatever way that He—not you—deems best. After all, God knows the evil that they've done, and He knows the proper way to handle them.

You can also pray that they realize the error of their ways. If they're engaging in some kind of bad behavior, you can ask God to change their hearts. Or you can pray that God gives *you* the grace to stop disliking them so much; that God heals you and helps you to forgive them; that God gives you the strength and confidence to relinquish your pain and trust in *His* justice.

If you can't do even *that*, then your hatred has gone so far that it really has separated you from God. Remember, God wills good for everyone—even those who are evil. Yes, God ultimately brings them to justice, but He doesn't hate them. He wants them to be saved. As the Bible says, God makes the rain fall on the good and on the bad (Matt. 5:45). And we're called to be in union with God—to imitate Him. So if certain people cause you to despise them so much that you're no longer able to do what God wants you to do, those people have effectively separated you from Him.

Is that something you really want to allow them to do? Think about it—someone wrongs you, and on top of the original crime, the person also causes a rift between you and God? Now you're letting that person harm you even more! That's something you simply can't permit. You can't give anyone—especially your enemies—the power to interfere with the *most important thing in your life*: your relationship with the Lord.

And there's really no reason to. Once again, forgiveness is not a feeling. When Christ was hanging on the Cross, He said, "Father, forgive them; for they know not what they do" (Luke 23:34). He didn't feel good at that moment. How could He? He was gasping for air and bleeding to death. He was in agony. His friends had abandoned Him, and almost everyone around him was mocking Him, spitting on Him, and cursing Him. There's just no way Christ could have *felt* very friendly or forgiving as He was being crucified. But that didn't stop Him from making the decision right there and then to pray for the people who were persecuting Him. When He was suffering most, He made sure He didn't exclude *anyone* from His love or His prayers or His forgiveness.

And neither should you. Forgiveness is one of the most essential parts of the Christian faith. You can't even pray the Our Father if you're unwilling to forgive others. Think about what that prayer says: "Forgive us our trespasses as we forgive those who trespass against us." When you say those words, you're basically asking God to forgive you in the exact same way that you forgive other people. So if you can't forgive your mother-in-law or your sister or your cousin because they've done something bad to you, then you can't expect God to forgive you either. He's going to treat you the same way you treat others. In fact, when you pray the Our Father in an unforgiving state of mind, you're actually asking God *not* to forgive you!

And guess what? He won't!

Do you think that's cruel? It's not. It's the only way God can be fair. There's a great parable in the Gospels that illustrates this point perfectly (Matt. 18:23–35). It's about a servant who owes his master a tremendous amount of money—the Bible says "ten thousand bags of gold" (Matt. 18:24, NIV), but in today's currency it would probably be something like nine million dollars. The master demands payment, but the servant begs him on his knees to give him more time. The master, a merciful man, is moved to pity and forgives him the entire debt. Naturally the man is overjoyed, but on his way out of the master's house, he happens to run into a fellow servant, who owes him one hundred silver coins—in today's money, a mere fifteen dollars. The man grabs his fellow servant by the neck and demands to be paid what he's owed. The servant begs him to be patient, but the man is ruthless. He actually throws the servant into prison until he can repay the debt.

Now, when the friends of the servant hear about this, they're outraged. They go to the master and tell him what has happened. The master, seeing how unmerciful his servant has been, unleashes all his fury on him: "You wicked servant," he says. "I cancelled that debt of yours because you begged me to. Shouldn't you have had mercy on your fellow servant, just as I had on you?" And in his anger, he hands the man over to the jailers to be tortured.

So what does this story mean? Obviously, it's about us—it's about you and me! We're the ones who owe our Master, God, a tremendous debt—in fact, an infinite debt. God gave us our very lives. We can't ever pay Him back for that. And instead of being grateful to Him, how do we act? We disobey Him all the time, don't we? In fact there's no end to our disobedience. And yet, as we saw yesterday, whenever we ask God for forgiveness, He grants it. He not only welcomes us back with open arms, but He offers us eternal life in Heaven. In other words, God gives us everything *and* forgives us everything.

Meanwhile, when our "fellow servants" sin against us, what do we do? We throw the book at them! We refuse to forgive them. We put a big X on them. Sometimes we even wish them cancer and everlasting damnation. "To Hell with them," we say. Don't you see? *We're* the wicked, unmerciful servants in the parable. We're the ones who have been forgiven a nine-million-dollar debt and then refuse to forgive the measly fifteen dollars that's owed to us! It's really incredible.

Well, how do you think God is going to treat us for acting this way? In the Gospel story, the master hands the man over to the torturers. That sounds pretty harsh. But in truth, that's exactly what happens to us when we become hardened by unforgiveness. We cut ourselves off from God and all His graces. Therefore, we cut ourselves off from the possibility of healing and from the peace and happiness that come from healing. Essentially, we hand ourselves over to torturers of a different kind—torturers of fear and loneliness and alienation and boredom and stress and anxiety and depression and frustration. When we purposely separate ourselves from God, that's the kind of life we're doomed to live, irrespective of how much money we make or how much success we achieve.

Once and for all, we're called to forgive everyone who sins against us, every time they sin against us. We're called to forgive *all* sins—even the most painful ones. We're called to forgive people even if they never ask us for forgiveness, even if they're not sorry, and even if they *keep* sinning against us. We're called to be *perfect* in our forgiveness.

Is that hard to do? Of course it is! In fact, it's impossible, humanly speaking. But remember the old saying "To err is human, to forgive, divine"? That's a statement of fact. Forgiveness really is divine. It's from God. And we know that nothing is impossible for God—*or* for us when we're acting in union with God.

So before you go on to the next section of this book, my suggestion is this: Why not try being divine for a change? Why not wipe the slate totally clean? Why not unload all the baggage of unforgiven sins that you've accumulated over the years? Why not make a decision here and now to forgive everyone who has ever hurt you?

Once you do that, I guarantee you'll be surprised by the burden of weight that will have been lifted from your shoulders. And when you try to flap those two wings we talked about earlier, you'll be amazed to see how easy it is to achieve takeoff.

Action Items

- ✓ Try hard to recall anyone who has ever injured you and then make a list of those people. On top of the list, write the words: "With God's help, I decide to forgive:"

  Remember, this isn't a decision to like these folks or even to associate with them again. It's a decision to forgive them—to wish them salvation and Heaven.

- ✓ Once you've finished forgiving every person you have a grievance against, sign and date the list.

The Meaning of Prosperity

Over the years, I've read dozens of self-help books and hundreds of spiritual books, and I can tell you that they all agree on one point. They all insist that it's impossible to be happy in this life if you don't first know how to be grateful for the blessings you already have. As the great Roman statesman and philosopher Cicero once said, gratitude truly is the "parent of all virtues."

Now, why would all these books and authors and philosophers agree on this point? People hardly agree on anything, and yet there's somehow common ground when it comes to gratitude.

I'll tell you why. It has to do with the nature of happiness.

I've used the word "happiness" a lot in these pages, but I want to clarify here that happiness isn't at all equivalent to "pleasure." That's why there's not a very strong connection between pleasure and gratitude, while there *is* between happiness and gratitude. It's possible for you to be extremely ungrateful and still experience many of life's pleasures. In fact, if you're an ungrateful type of person, I'd be willing to bet that you *have* experienced many pleasures. It's one of the ironies of life that the least grateful people often lead the most hedonistic lifestyles. They almost become professional pleasure seekers, going from thrill to thrill, searching for that one high that will finally satisfy the deepest yearnings of their souls. Only they never find it, because they don't have the faintest notion of what real happiness is all about. In the end, all the pleasures they experience do them no permanent good and lead them only to greater emptiness and despair. It's very sad.

Though they might not realize it, the main reason these pleasure seekers don't have the ability to be happy is that they're not humble enough to appreciate the purest, most basic blessings of life, and so of course they can't appreciate all the other, secondary blessings—such as sensory pleasures. The fact never seems to dawn on them that merely multiplying pleasures doesn't solve anything—not when the real problem is that they don't know how to appreciate to begin with.

This isn't a difficult principle to understand. It's why we teach our children to say "please" and "thank you" whenever we give them things—so that they won't turn out to be ungrateful when they grow up. We want them to understand that they really don't have a right to receive nice things. Yes, we want to give them that ice-cream cone, but they don't have a right to it. It's not owed to them. They have to say "please" and "thank you" because they need to know that the ice-cream cone—and the video games and computer games and the tablet and the dolls and toys and the rest—are all *gifts*. We give them to our children out of love, out of a desire to make them happy, not just because they want them.

Now, what happens when we don't teach our children to be thankful? They come to *expect* everything, don't they? They come to have no appreciation for the gifts they receive. They come to think that whatever they want, they *deserve*, that whatever they desire is theirs by birthright. And Heaven help their hapless parents if they *don't* get what they want! Because that's when the crying starts—and the sulking and the whining and the tantrums. When children aren't taught gratitude, they become spoiled—spoiled little brats! Isn't that true? Haven't you ever witnessed the spectacle of a spoiled child throwing a tantrum when he doesn't get what he wants? It's not very pretty, is it?

Well, I hate to break this to you. But guess what most of us are? We're spoiled brats too—spoiled *adult* brats! And I'm not just talking here about the Millennials or the older Generation Z crowd who are famous for feeling "entitled." I'm talking about *all* of us. Sure, we say "please" and "thank you" sometimes—to other adults. But when it comes to being grateful for the most important things in life—for all the true blessings that are given to us by God on a daily basis—we act exactly the same as ungrateful children.

What I'm going to say now may sound like a cliché, but it's the most important cliché you'll ever hear: existence is a miracle—*a miracle!* To answer Shakespeare's famous question once and for all, "to be" *is* better than "not to be." By a long shot! And yet people have lost the wonder of existence. They don't really, truly appreciate it—and so all the wonderful things that exist in life have lost their meaning and power as well. G. K. Chesterton said that until we appreciate the fact that things *might not be*, we won't ever be able to appreciate the *things that are*. Until we see the background of darkness, we can't possibly admire the light.

Now let me ask you some questions. How did you *feel* two thousand years ago when the Roman Empire ruled the world? How did you *feel* a hundred years ago, before you were even a gleam in your parents' eyes? How did you *feel* just one moment before you were conceived?

You felt nothing, right? You thought nothing. You *were* nothing.

When you go about your usual routine every day and get caught up in the million tedious details of life, it's easy to forget this momentous fact. It's easy to slip into a mode of ingratitude. But you *can't* forget it. You mustn't allow yourself to forget it. You were once nothing, and now you're something. And being something is better than being nothing. Chesterton also said, "When we were children we were grateful to those who filled our stockings with presents at Christmas time. Why are we not grateful to God for filling our stockings with legs?"[5]

What I'm saying now is serious stuff! If you want to transform your life, you have to correct this problem. You have to stop being so forgetful of the greatest blessing in the world. You have to stop being so unappreciative to God for the greatest gift He has given you. In the Gospel of Luke, there's a story about Jesus healing ten lepers. These poor sick people were outcasts from society. They had to stand at a distance from everyone—including Jesus. So Jesus had to yell over to them that they should go to the priest and then they would be cured. Sure enough, they went and were healed instantly. How many of the lepers do you think came back to thank Jesus? Just one! And it wasn't even a native Jew. It was a Samaritan—another outcast member of society. When Jesus saw him, He said, "Ten were healed, where are the other nine? Has no one returned to give praise to God except this foreigner?" (see Luke 17:17–18).

Jesus didn't take too kindly to this lack of gratitude. And why should He? Would you? How do you feel when people are ungrateful to you after you do nice things for them—when they take your kindness and your generosity for granted? Let's say you gave someone in your family a thousand dollars, and he didn't even thank you. What would you think about him? Let's say you continued to give him a thousand dollars every day, and he still didn't bother to show his appreciation. You'd probably have some

[5] See "The Ethics of Elfland," in *Orthodoxy*.

choice words for him, wouldn't you? And you'd *definitely* stop giving him money.

Yet God not only gave you life in the first place, but He continues to give you life every single day, every single week, every single month, every single year—even when you ignore Him. I wrote about this in a book called *Ten Prayers God Always Says Yes To*, and it's worth repeating it here.

Did you ever think about all the factors that had to be aligned for you to be born? About all the millions of tiny details that had to converge at just the right time and just the right place for you to come into this world?

In any single act of sexual intercourse between a man and woman, approximately five hundred million sperm cells are deposited in the female. *Five hundred million!* And only one of those sperm cells is allowed entrance into the woman's ovum. At the moment of contact, when fertilization first occurs, the egg releases a chemical that closes off all other sperm. Every other sperm cell—having lost the great race for human life—dies.

Half a billion potential human beings, each one completely different from you, could have been born in place of you had not that one, unique sperm cell fertilized that one, unique ovum. In a very real sense, half a billion other potential human beings had to forgo life to make way for you. Half a billion other men and women, each with their own distinct physical traits—their own hair, eyes, and voices—and each with their own unique personalities, never saw the light of day, so that you could live. We don't often think of it this way, but each one of us has already won a race in which we were five-hundred-million-to-one long shots.

In fact, the odds against you were even greater than that. For not only did one particular sperm cell have to fertilize one particular egg in order to result in the person called you, but it all had to happen in an extremely short window of time. In any given month, there are only five or six days during which intercourse can result in pregnancy. Had your parents not engaged in sex during that short fertile period—or had they practiced contraception—no child would have been conceived.

In other words, if you were conceived on a Tuesday at 10:00 p.m., that is the only time in all of history that *you* could have been conceived. A different instance of sexual intercourse at a different time would have yielded a different person because each sperm cell contains an entirely unique genetic code. The chances of the same sperm cell (the one that produced you) beating all those other cells on totally separate occasions are infinitesimal.

When you throw into the equation stillbirths (1 in 160 pregnancies), miscarriages (1 in 4 pregnancies), and abortions (1 in 4 pregnancies), it's easy to see how stupendously lucky you were to be born at all. From a strictly statistical point of view, your presence on this planet is a miracle.

True happiness begins with gratitude for *life*. Everything after that is mere icing on the cake. Look, it's easy to be grateful and happy and filled with excitement when you're at a party celebrating or at a club drinking and dancing with your friends or on vacation with your family splashing in the ocean. But can you be filled with the excitement of existence just sitting alone by a window, breathing? That's the kind of gratitude you're after. That's the kind of gratitude that has transformative power. And if you don't attempt to at least understand this point, you can forget about happiness. You'll never be able to experience it. But if, on the other hand, you remind yourself of it every day, there's a good chance you'll be able to be grateful for the other blessings in your life too.

What blessings? I have a friend who was born with only one arm. She's amazing. She has managed to teach herself to drive a stick-shift car, golf, play the drums, and become a gourmet chef. I challenge you to spend one day of your life doing just your daily tasks with one arm. Try washing and brushing your hair, try dressing, try cooking and eating, try washing dishes—try twisting the top off a bottle of water! Go ahead and try. I dare you. In fact, I bet you'll give up before you even finish your morning bathroom routine. But I guarantee you'll have more appreciation for that second arm and hand you have—that "little" blessing for which you've probably never once in your life thanked God.

We *all* have blessings—even those of us who are suffering. Even those of us who are grieving. Even those of us whose lives have been filled with unfathomable pain. Try a little exercise. Put aside your problems for a second and take a quick inventory of all the good things in your life. I know it might seem corny to do this, but go ahead and do it anyway.

Do you have your health, for instance? And by that I don't mean, are you free of ailments? I mean, can you sit up and breathe on your own, can you walk or move around on your own, can you see and hear what's going on around you? Are you able to eat? Do you have adequate food and shelter?

Do you have the gift of intelligence? Or any other talents? Are you free from serious mental or psychological problems? Are you able to read, to talk, to ask questions, to learn things?

Do you have any family or friends? Anyone you love or who loves you? Have they ever taught you anything? Have they ever done anything kind for you? Have you ever laughed and had fun times with them? What about animals? Have you had any pets? Have you ever been the recipient of the unconditional love of a dog?

What about all the experiences you've had—good and bad? Have they taught you anything? Have any of the really bad experiences ever led to anything positive?

What about the country where you've grown up and lived? Do you have rights there? Are you protected by laws? Are there doctors and hospitals in case you get sick? Are there police and firefighters in case you're in danger?

How about all the comforts of life? All the wonders of technology? Have you benefited from the advances that have been made the last hundred years—from antibiotics and anesthesia and pain killers to cell phones and computers and the Internet and electronic gadgets to all the other modern forms of convenience and travel and entertainment?

What about the beauties of nature? Have you been blessed by them? Not just sunsets and mountains and waterfalls and lakes and beaches and oceans but also the fields of study associated with all the natural sciences—such as botany and biology and physics and astronomy. Have you ever gotten any enjoyment from simply learning about the world?

And finally, what about all the quiet blessings in life? C. S. Lewis often talked about the joy of simply taking a walk in the woods, or reading a good book, or drinking a cup of hot tea on a winter's night. Ernest Hemingway wrote about the pleasure of just sitting at an outdoor café, watching the light change at twilight.

All of these are blessings from God. And all of them should be appreciated for what they are: freely bestowed gifts.

But there's even more. Gratitude doesn't pertain just to *natural* things. It has a spiritual dimension too. God has given us *supernatural* blessings that are even greater than food, family, and friends.

As Christians, we believe that by virtue of Christ's sacrifice on the Cross, we've become the adopted children of God. We're not just intelligent animals, high up on the evolutionary food chain: we're actually sons and daughters of God. That means we share in God's life—God's divine, *immortal* life. It means we can love with the same kind of love God has—a superhuman love. It means we can have superhuman faith and hope. It means that even if our lives are full of turmoil, we can have a peace that the Bible says "transcends all understanding" (Phil. 4:7, NIV).

It means that when we sin, we can be forgiven—easily; it means that God's mercy is always available to us, no matter what we do. So often Christians take this for granted. They take Christianity itself for granted. They don't realize what a privilege it is to have the true faith, to belong to Jesus Christ, to be able to know God intimately and personally through His Son and through His Word and through His Church.

Most important, they take it for granted that we've been given the possibility of eternal life with God. Christians believe in the resurrection. That means that someday we're going to rise from the dead—actually *rise from the dead*. All the things we desire now—money, power, status, fame, luxuries—are nothing in comparison with the joy that awaits us if we go to Heaven. This isn't wishful thinking or fantasy. It's what Christianity is all about. Someday, in Heaven, we're really going to see our loved ones again, and we'll be able to live together with them in a place that's free from all pain and sickness and sadness—forever.

Do you think that's something to be grateful for? Yet it hardly ever occurs to us. Instead, all we do is complain, complain, complain about our terrible problems. And that's why we're like spoiled children.

So what's the solution? How do we flick on the "gratitude switch"? It's not always the easiest thing to do. After all, when you have a spoiled child, it can be quite difficult to "unspoil" him. It takes a lot of work and doesn't happen overnight.

In fact, sometimes God has to intervene and do something drastic. C. S. Lewis famously said: "God whispers to us in our pleasures, speaks in our consciences, but shouts in our pains. It is his megaphone to rouse a deaf world."[6]

Did you hear that? *He shouts to us in our pain!* In other words, God sometimes allows pain and suffering to enter into our lives just to get our attention. Once that happens, then we're all ears! Then we start praying. Then we start going to church. Then we start begging God. Then we start thanking God—finally! It's that old cliché: *there are no atheists in foxholes.*

Isn't that terrible? What's the matter with us that we have to be shaken out of our slumber of ingratitude by fear that something might be taken away from us? To quote Chesterton again: "It is the point of all deprivation that it sharpens the idea of value. . . . In this world, through some sickness at the root of psychology, we have to be reminded that a thing is ours by its power of disappearance."[7]

What a tragic Catch-22! We can't be happy unless we're grateful to God for existence and all our many blessings. But we can't seem to be grateful unless we think we're in danger of losing those blessings. We're not adequately grateful for life until the specter of a deadly disease is hanging over our heads. We're not grateful for our health until we get sick. We're not grateful for our sight until we're threatened with blindness. We're not grateful for the use of our limbs until we have to have a hip or knee replacement. We're not grateful for our material blessings until we're faced with financial ruin. We're not grateful for our spouse until there's a real threat of divorce and the loss of our children. And on and on, *ad nauseam.*

[6] C. S. Lewis, *The Problem of Pain* (London: Geoffrey Bles, 1940), chap. 6.

[7] G. K. Chesterton, "On Being Moved," in *On Lying in Bed*, quoted in "To Have and to Enjoy," *G. K. Weekly* (blog), February 6, 2008, https://chesterton.wordpress.com/2008/02/06/to-have-and-to-enjoy/.

Listen, there are two general ways a person can wake up in the morning. One is pleasant, and the other, unpleasant. The unpleasant way is that the alarm clock near your head goes off, jolting you out of sleep. Or maybe someone comes along and yells in your ear or even physically shakes you. We've all experienced that. It's not very nice. But the second, more pleasant way of waking up is that someone in your family might go into the kitchen and quietly begin preparing breakfast. Still in your dreams, you might hear the eggs frying and the bacon crackling on the stove. The delicious smell of coffee brewing might waft into your bedroom. Before you know it, you're opening your eyes, naturally, without the need for an alarm clock ringing or anyone yelling in your ear.

Which way do you prefer—the alarm clock or breakfast? In terms of what we've been speaking about in this chapter, the breakfast approach involves being grateful for God's blessings, *right now*, before they're taken from you.

That means being grateful for life and all its wonders: grateful for the oceans and the mountains and the rivers; grateful for the weather—the gorgeous spring days, the lovely winter snowstorms, and the beautifully melancholy rain showers; grateful for the infinite variety of people to form relationships with—people with different gifts, different personalities, and different ways of adding joy to your life; grateful for the art and music that surround you; grateful for answered prayers; grateful for your family and friends; grateful for love and sexuality; grateful for your Savior, Jesus Christ; grateful for the Church with all her beautiful sacraments, prayers, and liturgy; grateful for all your countless personal blessings.

Do you really want to wait for that blasted alarm clock to go off before you feel these things? Do you really want to wake up to gratitude by having someone shake you and yell into your ear? Is that being intelligent?

This isn't rocket science, folks! People who are prideful and arrogant are always getting angry because they feel that either their rights have been violated or they haven't been given what they feel they're entitled to. They're unhappy because they're never satisfied with anything. By contrast, people who are humble always feel grateful for what they've *already* been given. They don't think they're entitled to *anything* from God. So anytime God gives them something, they consider it a bonus; they consider it the cherry on the whipped cream.

That's the way you need to be. In fact, you've got to cultivate more than a cliché "attitude of gratitude." You've got to make gratitude the keystone to your entire life. You've got to make it your "philosophy of life." You've got to make it your business to be in a state of appreciation and wonder *all the time*.

How do you do that? First of all, you have to constantly ask yourself the question "What am I grateful for?" You need to constantly count your blessings. You don't necessarily have to go over a full, itemized list all the time, but every day you should at least ask yourself what you're *most* grateful for.

Second, you should force yourself to say "please" and "thank you" more—to God. Saying grace before meals is just the minimum. Most people don't even do that nowadays—especially when they're at restaurants—because they don't want anyone to think they're "religious fanatics." What cowards! Christians need to have more guts than that. Chesterton, who spent his whole life writing about gratitude, went even further and said a short prayer of thanksgiving before going to concerts, before reading books, before admiring sunsets, before sketching, swimming, walking, playing, dancing, and even before he put his pen to paper. Why not do the same?

Third, if you want to feel gratitude, you sometimes have to feel what it's like to do without. You have to occasionally deny yourself what you're legitimately permitted to do. In other words, you have to *fast*. We talked about fasting earlier. It's a powerful way to help you to appreciate the things in life that you take for granted. And I'm not just talking about fasting from particular foods. I'm talking about fasting from *any* activity that you enjoy—such as using social media or gossiping on the telephone or binge-watching your favorite series on cable TV.

In the same way, you should sometimes force yourself to *do* things that are somewhat inconvenient. If you have a dishwasher, for example, you should occasionally wash the dishes by hand. If you have a car, you should sometimes take the bus to work. I hear people say all the time that they need a bigger car because their family is growing. But that's not true. They don't *need* a bigger car. They *want* a bigger car. Just look at the poor woman with four kids down the street, piling onto the bus with bags and a stroller. Sure, it's great to have a bigger car—but only if you appreciate that it's better than having no car at all.

Let's get this point straight. A person may feel that it's absolutely necessary to own a smartphone or a second car or a big flatscreen TV. But that feeling does not prove that the smartphone and the second car and big flatscreen TV are necessities of life. It only proves that a person can get used to an *artificial* life. Human beings have an absolute need for shelter. An absolute need for food and drink. An absolute need for air, fire, light, and heat. An absolute need for love and companionship. *Those* are the true necessities of life that comprise the "daily bread" that Jesus said we should pray for in the Our Father. He didn't say anything about the other luxuries of modern society—luxuries that have been misidentified and mislabeled as necessities. The truth is that while luxuries can be wonderful and useful, they are still artificial extras. In fact, today's extras—the cars, smartphones, tablets, computers, dishwashers, and so forth—should leave us all intoxicated with gratitude. The fact that they don't is more evidence that we're a bunch of spoiled children.

Finally, and most important, gratitude should not only help you to *feel* good but should also inspire you to *do* good. If you really appreciate the blessings you've been given by God, then you should show it by trying to imitate Him more. In other words, you should *share* your blessings. If you have money, you should be giving some of it away. If you have a nice house, you should be inviting people over to show them hospitality. If you have a big SUV, you should be offering to help your neighbors transport their things when they're in a bind. If you have a vacation home, you should be letting your family and friends stay there when you're not using it. If you're lucky enough to have free time, you should be devoting a portion of it to lending a hand in your community. If you have any special talents, you should be putting them to use in the service of others who don't have them.

The point is that you can't be stingy with the blessings God has given you. You have to show your gratitude by being kinder, more patient, more hospitable, more generous, more forgiving, more loving, more sacrificial. In a word, you have to act more like a true Christian!

Yes, I know that all of this is easier said than done. But it's necessary. Gratitude always results in happiness. That's a spiritual law as true and sure as any law of physics. And the opposite is also true: ingratitude always results in misery. Therefore, expressing gratitude to God every day is something you absolutely must begin doing if you want to turn your life around. A wise man once said that the worst moment in the life of an atheist is when he feels truly grateful for something but then realizes he has no one to thank. Fortunately, you and I don't have that problem. We know whom to thank. We just don't thank Him enough.

So why not fix that problem right this second? From now on, stop acting like a spoiled brat! Stop waiting for the alarm clock to wake you up! Make a decision to give up expectation, which always disappoints, and trade it in for appreciation, which always rewards. Make a solemn pledge to be more grateful for *everything* you've been given in life, materially and spiritually. No matter what your problems, make a real effort to remember that you're *already* rich. You already have more than most people. You already have wealth and abundance. In fact, when it comes to the blessings of God, you're already a billionaire.

Action Items

- ✓ Make a list of at least thirty things in life that you are grateful for.
- ✓ What are the seven most important things on that list? For the remainder of this month (and hopefully forever after), review these top seven every day and give thanks to God for them.

Spiritual Gravity

A few days ago, we talked about the decision to ask God for forgiveness whenever we sin. But we didn't focus on any kind of practical strategy to deal with sin itself. That's a big subject—too big for just one chapter—but there is something we need to discuss now if we're going to make any headway in our attempt to attain earthly happiness, and it has to do with the concept of "gravity."

Once, when I was in third grade, there was a science fair at school, and all the kids had to put together their own projects and present them to the rest of the class. I wanted to be a doctor from an early age, and I also loved dinosaurs, so science was my best subject. But I had a big problem: I was lazy. So I kept procrastinating and procrastinating, and when the day of the fair finally came, I still hadn't done my project. On the morning of my presentation, I desperately tried to come up with something—anything—but my mind was a blank. Then, as I was walking through the schoolyard, I had an idea. I spotted a small, smooth rock lying on the ground next to the fence and put it in my pocket before going in to class.

All the other kids seemed to be thoroughly prepared. In fact, some of the science projects looked as if they had been designed by NASA engineers, complete with buttons and levers and lights and sound effects. Bear in mind this was before the whole computer-techno revolution, so it was very impressive. I remember sitting there as each of the students presented his or her work, and thinking to myself, "I'm really going to look like an idiot."

When my turn finally came, I went to the front of the classroom, pulled the rock out of my pocket, held it in front of me, and said as seriously as I could, "Class, this is just a small rock, but look what happens when I let it go." I then ceremoniously dropped the rock and let it bounce on the floor. I looked up and said even more ceremoniously, "Did you see what just happened? The rock I was holding didn't float up into the air when I dropped it. No. It fell to the floor. I have just demonstrated one of the most important principles in all of science: the law of gravity. If it wasn't for the law of gravity, all of you would fly out of your seats right now and shoot into outer space at incredible speeds."

That's exactly what I said—or words to that effect. Then I explained what I remembered from my own reading about gravity. I even told them the legendary story about how Sir Isaac Newton "discovered" gravity one day when he was sitting under an apple tree reading a book, and an apple suddenly fell from one of the branches above him, conking him on the head.

My "presentation" amused some of the kids, but my teacher wasn't fooled at all. She gave me an Incomplete for not doing my assignment properly. And of course she was right. Laziness should never be rewarded. But as the years passed, I've realized something interesting. I've realized that what I said to my classmates that day was actually very significant. In fact, decades after that embarrassing presentation, I find that I'm *still* talking about gravity. Gravity as a principle is so fundamental and so important that it transcends physics and has applications in philosophy, psychology, ethics, and even theology. And the reason is that all things in life—not just rocks—have a tendency to fall.

This is especially true when it comes to our efforts to be good and virtuous. As I've said already, human resolve can be pretty pathetic sometimes. We all know how easily we fall back into our old habits and vices, and how happily we revel in the mud. I'm not talking about the influence of the devil or demons or dark spiritual forces. We'll get to *that* later in this book. Right now, I'm just talking about the tendency human beings have to sink to their lowest level. I'm talking about *spiritual gravity*. Most psychologists and personal-development experts don't seem to get this concept. They attribute our moral setbacks to false guilt or neuroses or insecurities or a hundred other things. But they never hit the nail on the head. Only the major world religions—especially Christianity—have identified the problem for what it truly is: a universal tendency to sin, caused by something in our own human nature that's broken, tainted, and fallen.

Remember the story of Adam and Eve in the Garden of Eden? Our secular culture dismisses it as a silly myth. But it's not. There are many profound spiritual truths contained in that story. Recall that in the book of Genesis, God created the first man and woman and placed them in the middle of Paradise. At the time, there was no such thing as suffering or death. Adam and Eve were happy, and God gave them complete freedom to do anything they liked—except one thing. He forbade them to eat from a certain tree in the middle of the garden because He said eating its fruit would kill them. That's really the key point to understand. What God was essentially saying was that human beings were created to have a lot of freedom. But there are *limits* to that freedom. You can't do anything you want, anytime you want. That's not freedom at all—it's license.

Well, we know how the story ended. Adam and Eve chose to disobey God and eat the forbidden fruit. And it was because of that free, prideful decision that evil and suffering entered the world and were passed on to future generations of mankind. In rejecting God, our first parents lost everything that went along with being in union with God—including perfect happiness on earth—and what they gained was sickness, corruption, war, loneliness, old age, and death.

And they got something else, too: a weakened human will and a tendency to sin, which we just talked about. Theologians call it *concupiscence*, and unless you understand that every human is subject to it, you'll never grasp why simple self-improvement techniques and other forms of psychological therapy never seem to work permanently. No matter how motivated we may be to change for the better, and no matter how much progress we make, there's always a force trying to drag us down. There's always a crack in our moral armor. There's always a natural *disposition* we have to sin. It's part of our very nature, and it originated when human beings first fell from God's grace.

That's why humility is so important in the spiritual life. Having humility means that you understand how *vulnerable* you are to making mistakes. After all, you're a weak, sinful, fallen human being. You're not perfect, and you never will be. When you're truly humble, you're not surprised when you commit a sin—even if it's an extremely serious sin and even if you've never committed it before.

That doesn't mean you're not sorry or that you're not committed to changing. Of course you have to change. Of course you have to make progress and become more disciplined and more virtuous. Of course you have to firmly resolve to turn away from your sins. That's one of the prerequisites of being forgiven—the decision to try to stop your bad behavior. But at the *very same time*, you have to recognize that you're really just a puny, powerless human being and don't have any real strength apart from what God gives you when you're in union with Him.

Do you understand this? Do you understand that you have absolutely no power—except maybe the power to screw up—unless you're in union with God in some fashion? It's only because of God's help that anyone can accomplish any *real* self-improvement in life.

Believe me, if you fall into despair over some offense you've committed, it's a sure sign of spiritual pride. It's a sure sign that you think you're stronger than you actually are. If you were humble, you would never beat yourself up. Instead, you would *pick yourself up* and try your best not to do it again.

I can't say this strongly enough. When it comes to your moral failures, you've got to employ what Mother Angelica, the feisty little nun who founded the Eternal Word Television Network (EWTN), called the "D and D" system—"do it and drop it." You've got to try with all your might to resist temptation, but if you give in and "do" it, then you've got to immediately say you're sorry and "drop" it. If it's a serious sin, then you should also resolve to go to Confession at your earliest convenience, but either way, you should never get too upset and never, ever lose hope in God's mercy. Remember, God has been watching human beings commit the same sins for thousands of years. There's nothing you can do that will shock Him. He has seen it *all*.

Now, of course, the best thing to do when faced with any kind of immoral temptation is to stomp it out before it gets too strong. And this is another point I want to talk about. It might seem obvious, but all "big" sins in life start out very "small." A tiny decision to engage in some "harmless" flirtation at the office can put a process in motion that eventually leads to an extramarital affair. A little "fudging" on the books to avoid an embarrassing financial situation can eventually lead to tax fraud. A choice to keep brooding over a frustrating family problem can lead to a terrible outburst of anger and a rupture in family relations. A decision to have one beer when you know you have an alcohol problem can result in a month-long binge and the loss of your job.

Every decision to do something wrong, no matter how small, has a moral trajectory of its own and the potential to lead to a much bigger problem. And if you fall in a serious way—for instance, if you commit adultery, steal from someone, or violently lose your temper—it's always the result of many smaller falls that took place beforehand.

So if you want to avoid the big falls, you've got to work on those smaller ones first. Doesn't that make sense? If there's an intruder at the door, and he wants to come in and hurt you, you've got to keep the door locked and bolted. The moment you open it—even an inch—you've given the intruder a chance to force his way in. And the more you open it, the harder it is to keep it closed; the harder it is to resist the power of the intruder as he pushes his way through. The only way to prevent a break-in is to stop it at the beginning. Or as Tony Robbins used to say, you have to "kill the monster when it's little."

If you don't, it can lead to all kinds of problems—not only bigger sins, but habitual sins as well, and compulsions, and even serious addictions. Anyone suffering from an addiction—whether it's drugs or alcohol or gambling or sex—knows how much havoc it can wreak in a person's life. Addictions can destroy your health, your self-esteem, your family and friendships; they can sap all your energy, rob you of your emotional and spiritual power, and cause you to waste years and even decades of your life. They're deadly in every way.

Have you ever seen a gerbil running on one of those spinning wheels? Sometimes people who have addictions feel just like that.

Once they start to binge—once they get caught on that wheel of compulsion—it's almost impossible for them to stop. Either they have to be thrown off because of some huge problem that their behavior has caused, or they literally fall off from exhaustion. Then they go through the same cycle again—bingeing, getting into trouble, breaking down from guilt or exhaustion, recuperating for a time, and then starting over.

It's a terrible way to live. Sometimes these poor people really sink into despair. They think God hates them and could never forgive them for their sins. But of course God loves them and is always eager to forgive them. He understands them and their compulsions better than they understand themselves; He knows that in many instances, they aren't giving the full, free consent of their will when they fall into temptation. He knows they're being *compelled* by their own habit, and so He forgives them when they're sorry—even if they fall a million times.

But that doesn't change the fact that addictions cause damage. Yes, God's mercy is infinite, and He'll always help in the healing process that follows a person's falls, but He isn't going to completely erase the destruction that has been done. And He won't restore the precious time that has been lost in the person's life.

For these reasons and more, if you've got some kind of unhealthy compulsion or addiction, you've got to make it your first priority in life to seek professional help—*now!* You can't wait another week or even another day. It's beyond the scope of this book to solve these kinds of problems. In fact, you can follow all the advice this book has to offer and still be unhappy if you have a serious addiction and fail to deal with it. You've simply got to bite the bullet and find someone who can help you. In this digital world of ours—this "information age"—there's no excuse not to. You're literally one click away from expert assistance for any problem you may have—many times at absolutely no cost. All you need is Internet access, and that's available free of charge in libraries and many other gathering places across the country.

Here's just one example of a practical tip you can learn by going on the Internet. Have you ever heard of the acronym "HALT"? When compulsive cravings strike, psychologists tell us that the four most common triggers are hunger (H), anger (A), loneliness (L), and tiredness (T). If you experience any of these states for long periods of time—and you have a tendency to compulsive behavior—then those compulsions are very liable to flare up. In other words, each one of these four conditions, if not dealt with, can make you vulnerable to addictive relapse. On the other hand, if you address these conditions—the hunger, the anger, the loneliness, and the tiredness—then the compulsive cravings will often begin to melt away. Not all the time, but often.

Even if you don't have an addiction, you know this is true. Haven't you ever wanted to bite off someone's head just because you hadn't had your lunch and were feeling grumpy? Or because you hadn't gotten enough sleep the night before? Or because you were angry about an unrelated problem with your boss or your spouse?

Of course you have. We all have. But if you suffer from a serious compulsion or addiction, then you have to be even more careful to avoid these vulnerable states. The result might not just be that you snap at someone. The result might be that you go on a binge; that you start running on that terrible wheel of compulsion again, with drugs or alcohol or gambling or sex or whatever it is you habitually use to obtain relief and pleasure.

The bottom line is that you have to keep the word "HALT" in mind at all times. You have to make sure you don't go for long periods without eating when you're hungry; you have to deal with any unresolved problems in your life that might be making you angry; you have to reach out to other people and get involved in different social activities in order to avoid being alone; you have to do everything in your power to get enough sleep and rest. In other words, you have to make sure you're taking good care of your *physical and emotional needs.*

And that's just the beginning. Not only do you have to employ these practical tactics, and not only do you have to seek professional help, but you also have to make use of all the grace God has to give you—through prayer, fasting, and the sacraments of His Church, some of which we'll be discussing soon. Any way you look at it, though, it's going to be a tough, uphill battle. But there's no way around it. You *must* commit yourself to doing it.

So let me try to summarize what we've said here very briefly.

No matter what you accomplish in life, no matter how successful or wonderful you become, you have to understand that there's always going to be a force trying to pull you down, a powerful spiritual gravity. It's just part of our fallen human nature. You have to recognize this tendency to sin, be humble about it, and never lose your self-esteem because of it. Life is going to be a moral struggle for you and everyone else you know to the very end—and you're going to have to be willing to fight, fall, repent of your sins, and get back up again many times.

When you do get back up, you're going to have to resolve that the next time you're faced with temptations—even tiny ones—you're not going to wait till later to deal with them. You're going to squash them right away, while you can still overpower them. You're going to slam the door shut on any potential threat. You're going to treat even the smallest sins as if they were deadly spiders—no more thinking, no more hesitating. Stomp on them and kill them—before they kill you!

Finally, if you do find yourself in the unfortunate position of suffering from a compulsion or an addiction, you're not going to lose your self-worth and self-esteem. You're going to HALT, take a deep breath, look at your life, and try to address any underlying emotional or physical problems that might be fueling the addiction. Most important, you're not going to be too prideful to seek professional help or too pigheaded to utilize the spiritual graces available to you. You're going to resolve to be strong and fight this addiction, not by yourself but with the help of family, friends, experts—and God Almighty.

Action Items

- ✓ Think about all your sins, bad habits, evil tendencies, and compulsions. Which one has the most power over you? Which has the ability to make you fall the quickest? Once you identify it, write down how you intend to deal with this problem the next time it shows up in your life. What action are you going to take to stomp it out before it grows so strong that you won't be able to resist and give in to temptation?
- ✓ If you have an addiction, what step can you take *now* to seek professional help? Even if you've sought help in the past without success, have confidence that this time will be different. I don't mean that your addiction will be conquered by the end of the book. Far from it. Some addictions take years and even decades to overcome. But the path you are on now is not the one you're used to. Very soon, I'll be giving you additional spiritual tools and weapons that will help you to win your battle. So go online, research where you can get help for your addiction, and make that first phone call.

Goals and God's Will

It has been said that there are three types of people in the world: those who make things happen, those who watch things happen, and those who *wonder* what happened.

Which category do you fall into?

You don't want it to be number two or three, do you? And yet that's where the bulk of humanity usually ends up spending most of its time.

How do you avoid it? The personal-development industry says the answer is to set goals for yourself so you can accomplish great things and "make your dreams into reality." And that's good thinking—as far as it goes. There's a tremendous amount of common sense behind the philosophy of goal setting. So many people have no clue what they want in life, much less how to go about getting it. They really are like ships drifting aimlessly on a vast ocean, floating wherever the prevailing wind happens to take them. Then there are folks who *do* have a general idea of what they want but never get around to the hard work of making their vague desires into specific, achievable objectives. They forget a very simple rule in life: you can't hit a target if you don't have a bull's-eye.

Goal setting gives you that bull's-eye to aim for. Unfortunately, there's a problem with it—a problem the personal-development industry, predictably, never brings up. And if you've been reading these chapters closely, you can probably guess what I'm about to say next.

As you carefully map out your own goals, you also have to consider what *God's* goals for you might be. God is already in the future. He already knows what will fulfill you—and what won't. Without taking His will into account, you're working on only half the equation. That's why so many people who achieve "success" are still unhappy. That's why so many people who are rich and famous commit suicide. Why would they kill themselves if they had realized all their glittering goals? Obviously, their goals didn't make them happy. They got caught in the world's trap. They followed their plan instead of God's. They forgot the main rule of all goal setting: Your dream is not necessarily your destiny. Your destiny is the thing God wants for you. It's the thing that will give you the most purpose, the most meaning, the most happiness, the most fulfillment.

The question is: What's the best strategy for setting your goals while taking your destiny into account—a strategy that's both humanly effective and spiritually intelligent? How do you combine the two? There are plenty of books and Internet resources available as well as workshops and seminars you can take. But what I'd like to do now is give you the basic principles of goal setting. To my mind, there are really only four.

The first and most basic rule is one that's going to sound almost laughably cliché. But it's the key to everything. You have to come up with goals that *inspire* you. Your goals have to be big enough, interesting enough, and exciting enough to make you really *want* to achieve them. Why is that so important? Because life is tough!

Because there are so many obstacles to overcome. As I said before, spiritual gravity is always trying to pull you down, trying to wreak havoc in your life. There's just no way you're ever going to accomplish anything significant if you're not willing to endure some real suffering and make some real sacrifices. And the only way to do that is to be motivated enough to make it through the pain and tedium and adversity that you're bound to face. So the idea is to find goals that are powerful enough to *pull* you into the future, rather than ones you have to get behind and *push* over what is sure to be a long, bumpy, uphill road.

This is so important. When I was younger, I used to think that people lived from pleasure to pleasure; that pleasure was the biggest motivator in life; that people constantly needed to have something concrete and tangible to enjoy in order to be happy and that these pleasures would inspire them to work the hardest and go the farthest distance. But I was wrong. In reality, people don't live from pleasure to pleasure. They live from hope to hope. As I've gotten older, I've come to appreciate the *power* of hope. Being able to look forward to something—even something small—is often enough to stave off serious depression in most people. Imagine how much more important it is when formulating objectives that you have to expend blood, sweat, and tears to achieve. Hope (and fear) are the things that drive people the most. That's why you simply can't have lame goals—goals that are impotent and unexciting. They have to be goals that instill in the deepest part of your being real hope for the future. Otherwise, they won't work.

Now, in order to come up with goals that inspire and fire you with hope, you've got to ask yourself some serious questions—and you have to be honest about the answers. What is it that you really want to achieve in life? What is it that you really love? What is it that gives you the most joy? What is it that gives you the most peace? Forget about what the world says you should want. Forget about what's "best" or "most impressive." You have to be brutally honest. What is it that you truly desire in your heart of hearts?

If you're able to come up with a few concrete answers, at least you'll have some indication of what God *might* want for you. God often plants intense desires in our hearts to help lead us where He wants us to go. You can't always be sure they're from Him, of course, but if you sincerely get joy and fulfillment from doing something, and it's not sinful, or detrimental to your state in life (as a married person or a parent or a member of the clergy), then it might very well be a sign that God wants you to explore the area more.

The second principle of goal setting is that you have to write all these things down and put them in a place where you'll remember to look at them. That's a more important step than you may realize. Most people today don't have written goals at all, and the ones who do usually look at them only once a year—on January 1. Then they put them in a drawer and don't look at them again till the following year. But what if you instead reviewed your goals every single day? Don't you think that would make a big difference in terms of how many of them you end up achieving? Of course it would. Just reading them at regular intervals will cause you to move toward them. Knowing clearly what you want—and why—will sharpen that inner, subconscious GPS that all of us possess. It will help you to immediately recognize situations and opportunities that might bring you closer to getting what you want.

There's something in life called "good pressure." It's not the same thing as anxiety, which is always debilitating and useless. Good pressure is when you see that there's a gap between where you are now and where you should be in life. Seeing that gap is often the best way to motivate yourself to *close* it. Yes, it's pressure, so it doesn't always feel good, but unlike anxiety, it results in movement and not paralysis.

Imagine for a moment being lost at the bottom of some desolate valley and looking up to the top of a mountain. If the valley was covered with dense clouds and fog, you wouldn't be able to get out. You'd be trapped there. But if it was a bright, sunny day, and you saw the direction you had to go and the distance you had to travel, you could make that journey up the slope to freedom. Writing down your goals and looking at them frequently is the same thing as clearing all that fog out of the valley of your mind. Yes, it's true that the distance you have to go might seem daunting at first, but the *clarity* of mind more than compensates for it. It's what makes the climb possible.

And that brings us to the third goal-setting principle: taking action. If you want anything meaningful in life, you have to work at it. Vince Lombardi, the famous football coach, said that the only place where success comes before work is in the dictionary. And it's true. God is not about to drop something magnificent into your lap simply because you happen to desire it. He just doesn't do that. Sometimes overly spiritual people think that all they have to do to get what they want is pray for it. But that's nonsense! You have to pray *and* work in order to achieve anything that's worthwhile.

Remember, Jesus Christ didn't save the world just by praying. Sure, He prayed a lot, but He also spent a great deal of His time *acting*. Read the Gospels and see if I'm lying. Christ was always healing people, performing miracles, preaching to the crowds, moving here, there, and everywhere. In other words, He was always working. He was always busy doing His Father's will. And if *He* had to work hard in order to accomplish His objective, then we're going to have to do the same for all our objectives. Doesn't that make sense?

So when you go about setting your goals, you always have to create a list of action steps to go along with them. I can't tell you what those steps should be because I don't know your goals. I can only tell you to consult with people you trust and people who have already achieved similar goals. I can only tell you to do your research and avoid reinventing the wheel. I can only tell you that you need to take as much action as possible—and that you need to start immediately after you set your goal, in order to build momentum. You've simply got to get that steamroller moving if you're going to overcome all the obstacles that will inevitably be thrown in your path.

Perhaps the two most important things I can tell you about taking action, though, are the following. In fact, they are so important that you can use them as guiding principles for your entire life:

1. In every situation you find yourself in, whether it's at work, in a marriage, in a family, in a friendship, in a business, or even in a simple everyday conversation, insofar as it's possible, *always be the person who adds the most value*. Remember, Christ said that anyone who wants to be first must be last of all and *servant* of all. He knew what He was talking about! Therefore, always be the one who gives the most. Always be the one who contributes the most. Always be the one who loves the most. If you do that, the people around you—even the ones who are jealous at first—will help guide you to the next level, to the place you need to be, the place you're *supposed* to be. In other words, they will assist you in achieving your goals, whether they are aware of it or not.
2. In order to be the person who adds the most value to every situation, you have to *work on improving yourself*

> *every day*. And doesn't that make sense? To *give* the most, you have to *have* the most. Therefore, you should always be trying to increase your knowledge about different subjects, always trying to learn new skills, always trying to discipline yourself, always trying to improve your energy levels, always trying to control your negative emotions, always trying to be more appreciative and cheerful and humorous and kind and understanding and forgiving. Like a great chef, you always have to be sharpening your knives. Of course, you don't have to do it all at once. This is something you do little by little, step by step, slowly but consistently over a long period of time. The bottom line is, don't waste so much money on *things*! You have too many things already! Instead, spend your money on ways to improve yourself so you can better assist others, so you can become the person who gives the most. Do that day after day, week after week, month after month, year after year, and believe me, everything else will fall into place.

The fourth and final goal-setting principle is by far the most important. It has to do with what we mentioned at the start of this chapter about God's will. I can tell you with 100 percent certitude that if you're praying constantly for God's guidance, that same God will inspire you with the best possible action steps to achieve your objectives. We've already said that God made the universe and everything in it, so when you're in union with Him, you're in union with the source of all creative power. You're actually tapping into creative genius. A human mind connected to God is like a giant supercomputer. If the goals you set are in line with what God wants for you, then when you ask Him in what direction to go, He's going to give you the answer.

Now, I realize it's not always easy to know what God wants. After all, He doesn't exactly hang up signs for us to read. In fact, He sometimes does the opposite. He sometimes plays hide-and-seek with us. He peeks His head out and shows Himself but then quickly darts around the corner and beckons us to follow. When we stop looking for Him, He usually comes after us—but even then, He always hides Himself for periods of time. That has been God's strategy since time immemorial.

When the apostles Andrew and John first met Jesus, they asked Him where He lived. And being God in human form, He didn't give them a straight answer. Instead, He said, "Come and see" (John 1:39). He does the same thing with us today. He doesn't give us the crystal-clear certainty we'd like to have. He gives us *glimpses* of the road ahead. The reason is that He wants us to seek Him. He wants us to search for Him. He wants us to pray to Him. He wants us to follow Him. He wants us to do all these things so we can draw into deeper union with Him. It's when we're in union with God that we're best able to discern what His will is for us—and for our goals. That's why we always have to include Him in all our major planning and decision-making. Not only will He help us go in the right direction, but if we start heading down the wrong path, He'll put roadblocks in our way that we *won't* be able to overcome.

That's such an important point to understand. Not every dream you have is God's will for you. As I said before, very often your dream is not your destiny. Lots of people dream about being artists or actors or musicians, but those dreams are the wrong path for them to take. God may have given them a powerful clue about their destiny—but that's just what it was, a *clue*. In order to draw us in closer to Him, God leaves it up to us to prayerfully discern the specific goal that His clues point to. He may place in the hearts of certain people the desire to be creative. But whether that God-given desire should ultimately be fulfilled through the performing arts, or the visual arts, or the constructive arts, or the medical arts, or any of the other arts in the world is not something God always spells out so clearly—at least not right away. It's something He leaves us to figure out. And many times, we can misinterpret God's clues, especially if we're not praying regularly.

Let me tell you a personal story to illustrate what I mean.

From the time I was a little boy, I wanted to be a doctor—specifically, a heart surgeon. That's all I wanted to be right up until college. And I might have succeeded, too, if it weren't for a few "little" things that got in the way—like organic chemistry, integral calculus, and girls!

When that didn't work out, I felt pretty bad. So I went back to another great ambition I always had: to be a writer. But I didn't know what kind of writer I wanted to be. I tried everything—political speeches, history textbooks, journalism—but none of it really inspired me. Then, sometime in my twenties, after years of being away from the Faith, I started to get more interested in Christianity. There were a lot of reasons for this, but mainly it had to do with some of the books I was reading and some of the people I was meeting. Anyway, I finally started praying to God to lead me in the right direction.

About that time, I took a trip to England and found myself on a train going north from London to Manchester. I had purchased a paperback copy of C. S. Lewis's well-known book *The Screwtape Letters* at the Westminster Abbey bookstore and began reading it as the train pulled out of the station. After just a few pages, I knew I was on to something important. The book made a powerful impression on me. It was the first time I had ever read anything spiritual that made me laugh and think at the same time. It was so cleverly written that I read the whole thing from cover to cover and then started over again right after I finished. I had never done that with any book before.

I had an epiphany on that train ride. I realized that maybe there was a way I could combine *both* of the great ambitions of my life. I realized that maybe God had given me the desire to be a doctor and the desire to be a writer for a reason. If I could write books like *The Screwtape Letters* (not anywhere as good, of course), perhaps I could still have what I always wanted. Perhaps I could still help people who were sick—not through surgery, but through writing.

That was a big revelation to me. For so many years, I thought I wanted to be a doctor. But I was wrong. My true desire wasn't to be a doctor at all—it was to be a *healer*. Like many other people, though, I had interpreted incorrectly the clues God had given me. I started to get the right interpretation only when I began to pray.

But that's not the end of the story. It turned out that even having the right interpretation wasn't enough. Ten years later, I *still* hadn't written any spiritual books. The reason was that my vague desire to be a writer was just that—vague. I hadn't really done anything about it. I hadn't created any plan. I hadn't combined my prayer with my God-given common sense and my ability to take action. So in my frustration, I decided to try something new. I decided to employ some rudimentary personal-development techniques I had learned from listening to a series of Tony Robbins audiotapes. Most important, I got serious about goal setting.

It was about this time that I took another train trip—this time from New York to Washington, D.C. I remember it was in the middle of a winter blizzard, and I took the slowest train I could find. For close to four hours, all I did was write out my goals. I had a steaming cup of coffee in front of me, and every so often, I would look out the window and watch the snow blowing onto the streets and houses as the train sped through the different towns. By the time I arrived in Washington, I had several pages of written goals, together with all my reasons for wanting to achieve them. Even more important, I had put my goals down in a *prayerful* way. Yes, I let my imagination run wild, but I did it with the strong conviction that I wanted to attain these things only if they helped bring me closer to God.

I decided on that train ride to write a book called *A Travel Guide to Heaven* and to do it within six months. I looked at my busy workweek, decided which blocks of time I would need to devote to writing, put them on my schedule, and got busy. It was very difficult for me to complete, never having written a book before, not having an agent or a publisher, and trying to hold down a full-time job at the same time—but with God's help, *I did it*. And it changed my whole life.

Twenty years and more than twenty-five books later, I tell you in truth that *you can do it too*! You can achieve whatever goals you set for yourself, no matter how big, as long as God is behind you and you aren't afraid to work hard and pray hard. That's the most effective combination in the world—and that's the combination you need to strive for. Even if you've had experience with goal setting, it's time to start fresh and try again—this time with an intelligent, written plan and the cooperation of God.

This can be a very important day for you! Be creative. Be daring. Be holy. Find some time to get away for an afternoon and focus on just this subject alone—and then start setting some inspiring goals. Include them in your daily prayers, persevere, and have faith that the same God who created you out of nothing can help you create a destiny for yourself more magnificent than your wildest dreams.

Action Items

- ✓ Get your calendar. Decide when you're going to take a few hours to work on your written goals. Can you possibly do it today or tomorrow? If not, make sure you schedule it on a day this coming week, *before* you finish this thirty-day program.

Rest, Review, Celebrate

Congratulations! You made it through Week 3! Only one more week to go!

If you have time to work on your goals today, that would be great. If not, take the day to review your accomplishments of the past week and celebrate them. If you did all the action items at the end of each chapter, this has been a truly momentous week for you—one in which you wiped the slate of your past life clean and started down a new path, hand in hand with God.

Remember, this is the Lord's Day, so be sure to go to church and give thanks to God for all that He is doing to help you. I'm hoping that by this time, you've decided to embrace your faith and even to take it to a new level. If so, ask God to bless that decision and help form it into a deeply held, lifelong commitment.

See you tomorrow!

Start Your New Life

The Fullness of Truth

Now that we've laid a good foundation, I want to get a bit more specific about the most important part of personal transformation: spirituality. You'll find that the next few chapters of this book are written from a more Catholic perspective. But first, I have a confession to make.

When I originally conceived the idea of this book, I thought it would be wonderful if I could write it for all people, whatever their faith or even if they had no faith at all—even if they were atheists. But I soon realized that was impossible. You know why? Because I didn't want to waste your time. Because then this would just be another personal-development book, and not only are there thousands of those on the market already, but as I've said repeatedly, personal development isn't enough. In order to be your best self, you need more than just self-help—you need God's help too.

So then I thought, maybe I could write this book for anyone who believed in God—no matter what their religion or spirituality. But I soon realized I couldn't do that either. For instance, lots of people today are flocking to Buddhism—especially the folks in Hollywood. They're attracted to Buddhism's seeming "looseness" and "tolerance," its lack of "rigid structure" and the "inner peace" it brings to their hectic lives. More times than not, of course, what they really like is the fact that Buddhism doesn't have all those annoying "thou shalt nots" that make it so difficult for them to be vain, selfish, and hedonistic without guilt. It's very convenient for the movie-star lifestyle!

Hollywood aside, though, there's much to admire in the Eastern religions. There's a lot of truth about life that can be learned from them. The real problem is, you can't accurately call them religions. They're much more like philosophies. Buddhists believe neither in a personal God nor in personal immortality. In fact, the whole idea of personal immortality is anathema to Buddhists. Buddhism is all about eliminating the self—not improving or perpetuating it.

There's a joke I like that conveys the essence of Buddhism:

What did the Buddhist monk say to the hot-dog vendor?

"Please make me one with everything."

One with everything. Exactly! That's what Buddhists want. That's what they're striving for in all their meditations and all their efforts at self-denial. They want to reach Nirvana—a state in which they'll have lost all sense of self, when all their human desires will have vanished. Once it was explained to me this way: Imagine that you're a drop of water and you're put into the ocean. The drop becomes part of the ocean; indeed, it becomes *one* with the ocean. That's the ultimate purpose of Buddhism.

And that sounds so nice, doesn't it? It sounds so peaceful and lovely. That little drop of water, dissolved completely, is now finally free in a sea of tranquility, free from all pain, at harmony with the universe. Such pretty-sounding words.

But do you know what those words mean?

They mean the drop is gone! What do you think happens to a drop of water when it's submerged in the ocean? It loses its identity!

It's no longer a unique, individual bit of water. Its identity has now become the identity of the ocean. For all intents and purposes, there is no longer any drop of water. It's gone forever. Kaput!

Is that what you want? To be gone forever? To lose your identity?

Well, that's what Buddhism teaches. And it's exactly the opposite of what Christianity teaches. According to Christianity, your identity is not something bad; it's something good, something sacred; it's something that's meant to live forever. Yes, it's necessary to connect with others, to be close to others, to love others, and even, at certain times and in a certain sense, to be "one" with others, but it's also necessary to be your own special self, to be a unique, precious, unrepeatable creation of God. We believe both these truths at the same time.

Christianity teaches self-denial and self-detachment too, but for a different reason than Buddhism does. Denying and detaching ourselves helps to strengthen our will, to increase our gratitude for the things we've denied ourselves as well as our gratitude for the God who gave them to us; to bring us closer to God and thus to make us even better *individuals*. The whole point of "losing ourselves" in Christianity is not to lose ourselves permanently because our nature is evil or because human desires result in suffering—but rather, to renew and transform ourselves. The whole point of dying to ourselves in Christianity is not to die permanently because life is bad but, rather, to die in order to experience resurrection—a resurrection to a new kind of life, a life worthy of the Kingdom of God.

In the end, God intends to help us become even *more* of who we are—to become our best selves, our divine selves, the selves God had in mind when He created us. And those selves are not destined to be annihilated in Nirvana; they're meant to come to fruition in Heaven. In Heaven we're meant to love God and to love others for all eternity—while at the same time retaining our individuality. That's the Christian understanding of life, and because of that understanding, personal development and "self-help" in this world are perfectly legitimate enterprises and completely compatible with our relationship with the Lord—as long as we make the Lord part of the process!

So, no, Buddhism and its idea of permanent renunciation of self doesn't quite fit into the program for this book.

But what about the other world religions? Specifically, what about all the many and varied denominations of Protestant Christianity? When I wrote the first version of this book, I did indeed want it to be for all Christians. I attempted to take a C. S. Lewis approach. I wanted everyone who believes in Jesus Christ to be able to use this book to help them overcome their problems. I think I might have even accomplished part of that objective. But again, I found that my efforts fell short of the mark. At some point, I saw I wasn't being honest with myself. I realized that to truly become your best self and to transform your life in the most effective, efficient, and powerful way, it matters very much whether you're a Mormon or an Evangelical or a Catholic.

Don't misunderstand what I'm saying. This is not a book of Catholic apologetics. I'm not interested in convincing anyone to be a Catholic with my clever arguments. That's for other, more skillful writers. But the fact of the matter is, no other belief system has more resources at its disposal to help you achieve self-mastery and self-renewal and self-transformation than Catholicism. No other belief system is as rich in history and intellectual and spiritual heritage as Catholicism. No other belief system has as many *sacraments*—channels of divine grace and assistance—as Catholicism. No other belief system has as much truth as Catholicism.

Yes, *truth*. Some people have trouble believing that any religion can be true, for the simple reason that there are so many different religions in the world. They find the sheer number of competing belief systems an obstacle to their having faith in any one of them. But these folks miss the point. The fact that there's a large number of religions doesn't logically prove anything. G. K. Chesterton had a good analogy for this. He said that in a horse race, you can have as many as twenty horses competing. And every single one of those horses has a following of thousands of people who believe in it—even to the point of placing money on that horse to come in first. Now, all those horses are in the same race, and they're all racing to the same finish line, but only one of them wins. Nobody ever says that because there are so many horses with so many bettors, none of them can possibly end up being first. There's always a winner, regardless of the number.

Or look at it a different way. You might ask a classroom of first graders, "How much is seven times seven?" You'd probably be amazed at the number of answers you'd get. And yet we know that there's only one correct answer: forty-nine. Do you see what I'm getting at? The fact that there's a whole slew of answers and beliefs and opinions doesn't prove that one of them isn't the right one.

But let's take the analogy further. If you asked those first graders, "How much is seven times seven?" and one of them said forty-two, he'd be wrong, but he'd be closer to the truth than someone who answered seventy-five and closer still than someone who answered five hundred. In other words, the answer one person gives can be *more* wrong than the answer another person gives. Conversely, some answers might not be exactly correct, but they may be a lot closer to the right answer than others.

It's the same with belief systems. Nobody is claiming that Buddhists don't have some of the truth. Of course they do! Nobody is saying that Muslims don't have some of the truth. Of course they do! Nobody is saying that Jews don't have some of the truth. Of course they do! Nobody is saying that all the different denominations of Protestantism don't have some of the truth. Of course they do! In fact, all Christians are a lot closer to the truth than Buddhists or Muslims or Jews, because they believe that Jesus Christ is Lord. They believe that He died in order to reconcile God to man. They believe that it's because of Christ's death and Resurrection that human beings can be saved and go to Heaven. That's a lot of truth!

But it's not all the truth. It's not the *fullness* of truth. If you want that, you have to go to the Catholic Church—the Church that Jesus Christ Himself founded.

But what about the scandals? you ask. What about the Inquisition? What about the Crusades? What about the bad popes? What about all the hypocritical Catholic politicians today? How can anyone trust a religion that has produced so many sinners?

Listen, my friend: Catholics—like everybody else in the world—have been guilty of committing great sins. If you want to discredit Catholicism on the basis of sinful Catholics, you can go back a long way. In fact, you can go back to the very beginning, to the very first followers of Christ. When you read the Gospels, you'll see that Jesus was frequently frustrated and even angry with the apostles. He always seemed to be a hair's breadth away from yelling at them. He was constantly disappointed by them. He was constantly saying things to them like "How long should I stay with you and put up with you?" (see Mark 9:19).

The apostles were a group of selfish, childish, small-minded, envious, angry, cowardly men. They were always complaining and bickering among themselves. They were always whining about how tired they were, how sleepy they were, how confused they were, how scared they were. They were always weak in their faith—even after Jesus had performed miracle after miracle in their presence.

They were actually a big bunch of babies—and keep in mind that these were the first bishops of the Catholic Church!

And what about Judas? He was one of the twelve apostles, too. He was hand-picked by Jesus Christ to be a bishop. And yet he betrayed the Lord—for money.

The point is, Catholics are used to this kind of behavior in the Church. We're well aware that the sinfulness of Catholics—including those in the Church hierarchy—runs very deep. I'm not saying that that's a good thing or that it should be excused. On the contrary, it's pathetic; it's painful; it's shameful; it's scandalous. It should be rooted out and destroyed wherever and whenever it's found. But it's nothing new. Jesus had to deal with it too. But despite the shortcomings of His disciples, He still thought the Church was worth founding.

What does this mean in terms of choosing the right religion to believe in? It means that if the sins of Catholics are going to stop you from being a Catholic, *adios, amigo*!

The presence of sinners in any religion doesn't demonstrate anything except for the fact that *all* of us need a savior. And cataloging the bad behavior of Catholics certainly doesn't demonstrate that Catholicism itself is bad. It proves only that humanity as a whole has a longstanding problem with evil and that a person's Catholicism doesn't override free will. Chesterton put it this way:

> The abuses which are supposed to belong especially to religion belong to all human institutions. They are not the sins of supernaturalism, but the sins of nature.... When people impute special vices to the Christian Church, they seem entirely to forget that the world ... has these vices much more. The Church has been cruel; but the world

> has been much more cruel. The Church has plotted; but the world has plotted much more. The Church has been superstitious; but it has never been so superstitious as the world is when left to itself.[8]

For goodness' sake, if you're going to make an informed judgment about Catholicism, look at *all* of its history—not just the bad parts. I wrote about this in a book called *Inside the Atheist Mind: Unmasking the Religion of Those Who Say There Is No God.* In that book I described the *good* the Catholic Church has done. I recounted how the Church gave the world the first university system, the first hospital system, and the first orphanage system. It has given the world hundreds of thousands of charities.

Don't believe me? Just do an Internet search for "Catholic charities" and see how many names appear. They're legion: missions to foreign countries, organizations to fight world hunger, inner-city soup kitchens, and ministries to assist those with every kind of infirmity. Think of Mother Teresa's Missionaries of Charity. Think of all the orders of nuns established to care for the diseased and the dying. Think of all the Catholic orphanages that have helped so many abandoned and destitute children over the centuries. Think of the thousands of Catholic hospitals that are in operation across the globe. There's simply no end to the number of charities founded by the Church.

We talked earlier in this book about some of the incredible contributions that the Catholic clergy has made to science—such as the big bang theory and the science of genetics. But the Church has also given the world some of the greatest artists, writers, and

[8] Quoted in Dale Ahlquist, *G. K. Chesterton: The Apostle of Common Sense* (San Francisco: Ignatius Press, 2003), 181.

philosophers—not to mention some of the holiest saints, most courageous martyrs, and most effective social reformers and social reform movements.

It was Catholicism that dramatically elevated the status of women when practically every other culture in the world oppressed them. That's right! Women's rights come from the Church! The ancient world treated women worse than dogs. Read the Greek and Roman historians if you have any doubts about that. Women were the property of men, barely higher than slaves. They had no rights at all. That's why they were so frequently exposed to the elements as infants. The Catholic Church changed all that. Women had leadership roles in the early Church. Instead of being abused, they were educated and protected. The whole medieval concept of chivalry arose because Catholic civilization considered women to be of a *higher* dignity than men.

The same can be said about slavery. Enemies of the Church are always claiming that because Catholics owned slaves at various times in history, the whole religion is hypocritical. But that's nonsense. Slavery was practiced for centuries all over the world before Christianity came on the scene. No one ever criticized or opposed slavery in any systematic way—*until* the first Catholics. From its very beginning, Catholicism discouraged the enslavement of fellow Catholics. And many early Catholics purchased slaves for the sole purpose of setting them free. Because human dignity is at the heart of Christian doctrine, it was only a question of time before Catholics began to realize that the very idea of "owning" another human being was contrary to their Faith. By the Middle Ages, the institution of slavery—which provided the whole foundation for Greek, Roman, and Egyptian civilizations—was largely replaced by serfdom, a system that at least guaranteed basic human rights to all workers—such as the right to marry and to own property. It was these efforts by early Catholics that set the stage for the first anti-slavery and abolition movements in Europe and in the United States.

Again, nobody is saying here that Catholicism is perfect or that it has been free of hypocrisy. It hasn't—not by a long shot. But in evaluating the cost-benefit ratio of anything, especially something as large as a religion, you have to separate individual examples of evil from the overall pattern of good. You have to look at the big picture.

Those who attack the Church love to go through history searching for "rotten fruit." When they discover some, they zealously rush to judgment without any real understanding of history itself. They look for dark specks on the vast canvas of history and, when they discover them, they conclude that the canvas itself is completely black—when in reality, it is astonishingly white.

Any fair-minded, thinking human being who looks at history with an unbiased eye has simply got to acknowledge that the contributions made by the Catholic Church to human rights, social rights, civil rights, arts, and culture far outweigh any harm it has done.

So please, if you want to make progress in transforming your life, don't reject Catholicism because of its history of sinners or because of all the ignorant arguments our enemies use against us. Instead, look at the incredible things Catholicism has done to change the world and then realize that the power it took to do that can also be harnessed to change *you*!

Ultimately, I had to write this book from a Catholic perspective because, regardless of the problems in the Church, it is still the "First Church of Jesus Christ," the Church that Jesus Christ founded upon the rock of the first pope, St. Peter. And even more importantly, in terms of the specific objective of this book—the

Catholic Church gives a person more tools, more weapons, more resources, more assistance, more grace, more power, more *everything* to turn his or her life around.

What are these tools the Church gives you? I'll explain shortly, but first, let's discuss all the people who are born Catholic but then leave the Church. Let's talk about lapsed Catholics. There are certainly a lot of them out there. Maybe you know some. In fact, maybe you're one of them!

Action Items

✓ Do a quick Internet search of Catholic charities. Then do a search of Catholic saints, Catholic scientists, Catholic philosophers, Catholic artists, Catholic musicians, and Catholic writers. These don't have to be in-depth searches. The idea is to get a more global perspective on the contribution that Catholicism has made to the world. Write down anything that you find surprising.

The Map of Life

Catholics who leave the Church: they seem to be all over the place. It's a very interesting phenomenon. These folks are baptized Catholic. They grow up Catholic. They attend Catholic schools. They're confirmed Catholic. They go to Church regularly in their youth and even get married in the Church. And then, for some reason, they leave.

Sometimes they leave for a "big" reason: perhaps they stopped believing in God, or maybe they were victims of sexual abuse by a member of the clergy. But most times, the reasons people leave the Church are much more mundane. They're no longer Catholic because they find the Mass boring. Or they had a bad experience in a meeting with their pastor. Or a priest was nasty to them in Confession. Or they don't like the pope. Or the Church just doesn't make them feel close to God anymore. Or the music down the street at the Lutheran church is better and the people there are friendlier. And on and on.

Many times, these fallen-away Catholics will shake their heads in dismay and trot out that tired old cliché "I just don't believe in organized religion."

If I had a dollar for every time I've heard *that* one!

As if there were anything wrong with being "organized." What if you needed bypass surgery and your cardiologist said to you: "I really love performing intricate, complex heart surgery, but I've never actually studied the procedure. I just go by feel." Or what if you wanted to have a home built and the engineer told you: "I have no degree in engineering, and I'm not familiar with the laws of physics, and I have no knowledge of architectural plans or plumbing or electricity—but constructing homes makes me feel so wonderful that you should trust me with the job." Or what if someone wanted you to invest in a business scheme and said to you: "I have no business plan, no budget numbers, no timetable, no organizational chart—but give me all your money anyway because my idea is really great."

Do you get what I'm saying? In every important area of life, there needs to be a certain level of organization; otherwise, there's disaster. You can't have a science of medicine unless it's organized; you can't have a system of laws unless it's organized; you can't have cities or houses or farms or movies or music or *anything* of value unless some facet of it is organized.

You can't have any kind of living body unless it's organized too—organized in its skeletal structure, its muscular structure, its internal structure, its circulatory structure, its neurological structure, its cellular structure. What happens when the body of a human being dies? It decays; it decomposes; it disintegrates; it *loses* all its organization and becomes putrefying mush! Well, what do you think the Church is? It's a living organism. And organisms need to be organized! You've heard this before in the Bible. St. Paul said that followers of Jesus Christ make up His "Body," and that this "Body" has many different parts and functions. Well, what do you think happens when the "Body of Christ"—which St. Paul specifically identified as the Church—loses its organization? Just like any other living body, it decays, it decomposes, it disintegrates—it dies.

"But hold on," comes the standard reply. "Isn't the most important thing to have a personal relationship with the Lord? Isn't that the only thing that really counts? And personal relationships don't have to be organized, do they?"

Yes, of course they do! That's the point so many people miss. Your relationship with God needs to be a profoundly intimate one. And it *is* the most important thing in the world. But that doesn't reduce the need for organization; it *increases* it.

Please try to understand this concept, which at first may seem counterintuitive. Any successful relationship has a built-in organization, a built-in structure, a built-in architecture; otherwise, it's doomed to failure. The organization of a long-lasting marriage may not be visible to the eye, but it's there: a delicate balance of responsibilities and obligations and expectations between spouses; boundaries that both individuals have in themselves and respect in their partner; unwritten rules that govern the relationship and ensure that the mutual love that powers it is channeled in the best possible way at the best possible time; a clear understanding of a million details relating to sex, child-rearing, bill paying, mealtimes, work times, house chores, family functions, in-laws, and so forth. In other words, there is a tremendous amount of organization in any relationship that works—even though it might not be immediately apparent. It's only those relationships with no organizational substructure (or a very loose, weak one) that *don't* succeed over the long term.

It's the same with our relationship with God. The fact that we know and love God and have faith in His Son Jesus Christ doesn't take away one iota from the fact that God still expects us to act in certain specific ways; that He expects us to follow certain specific laws; that He expects us to spread certain specific news about His Kingdom; that in order to help us meet those expectations,

He gives us certain specific kinds of graces that are distributed in certain specific kinds of ways. In other words, our relationship with the Lord is not something mushy and undefined and static and stagnant—it's something rich and complex and living and growing and *dynamic*. And any kind of dynamic activity requires organization.

But people don't want to hear that, do they? They want organization in everything under the sun except their dealings with God. They want organized hospitals. They want organized health care. They want organized mechanics. They want organized judges and juries. They want organized schools, organized banks, organized checkbooks, organized toolboxes, and organized makeup cases. But when it comes to *the most important subject in the world*, the one thing that's really, truly essential in their lives—their relationship with the Almighty Creator of the universe—all of that suddenly goes out the window! Then they don't want any organization. Then "organization" becomes a dirty word. Then organization somehow stops them from feeling *connected* to God. It gets in the way of all their mushy feelings. It threatens them.

How absurd!

Our relationship with God is a heck of a lot more than mushy feelings. As I said earlier in this book, feelings are by their very nature impermanent. Yes, I know they can be important. Yes, I know it's lovely to bubble over with enthusiasm when you think about God. It's delightful to feel that you're basking in the glow of God's love. It's easy to see why a person might walk down to the beach at sunset and marvel at the blazing colors and smell the fragrant saltwater air and feel the soft breeze caress his face and think to himself, "Ah, I feel so close to God right now."

Of course he feels close to God at that moment—because he's experiencing firsthand a reflection of God's beauty in one of God's most awe-inspiring creations. There's nothing more natural than feeling overwhelmed in the face of such magnificence. But what too many people do is jump to the illogical and totally erroneous conclusion that the good feeling they have on the beach is somehow more real than the experience they have in church; more real than the experience of receiving the sacraments; more real than the experience of saying their memorized prayers; more real than the experience of fulfilling all the humdrum daily obligations of their faith. The problem with these people is that their definition of "real" is screwed up. It's too tied to their emotions.

C. S. Lewis understood this point well. In his book *Mere Christianity*, he described how people often get muddled when it comes to identifying what's genuinely real in the world. He said that if a person looked at the Atlantic Ocean from the beach, and then went back home and looked at a map of the Atlantic Ocean, he might think that his experience at the beach was more real, while the experience of viewing the map was less real. But that would be a mistake:

> The map [Lewis said] is admittedly only colored paper, but there are two things you have to remember about it. In the first place, it is based upon what hundreds and thousands of people have found out by sailing the real Atlantic. In that way it has behind it masses of experience just as real as the one you could have from the beach; only, while yours would be a single glimpse, the map fits all those different experiences together. In the second place, if you want to go anywhere, the map is absolutely necessary.

Do you understand what Lewis is saying here? It's so important, especially if you're one of those people who has left the Church because you don't like "organized" religion. He's saying that, in many ways, looking at a map of the ocean is more important and even closer to reality than looking at the ocean.

And that's exactly what so many people fail to grasp. They're perfectly content to go through life looking at the ocean from the beach. That's what they *want* their religion to be like. It's so easy. It's so undemanding. It feels so good. Who wants to look at some "boring" old map? Who wants the trouble of examining all those tiny details, or trying to understand the big picture, or figuring out how to get from point A to point B? It's not always fun to do that. Looking at a map might involve work. So these people end up strolling leisurely along the beach their entire lives, pacing up and down the same stretch of sand, never really going anywhere spiritually.

But is that the point of your personal relationship with God? Is that the point of authentic spirituality? Is that the point of your faith in the Lord? To go in circles—endlessly? Or is the point to *do* something? To do God's will, not your will. To worship God on His terms, not your terms. To help family, friends, and strangers who are hurting. To be able to experience peace and joy yourself, even when things are not going well—even when you're not looking at a beautiful sunset on the beach—even when you're in a hospital bed suffering or at a funeral parlor grieving. To get to Heaven and to be as happy there as possible. To spread the good news about God and salvation and to assist as many other people as you can to go to Heaven *with* you.

We're not talking here about the age-old battle of faith versus works. We're a thousand miles away from that. We're not interested in defining in precise theological terms what's required for a person to be "saved." Sure, you might not believe in organized religion and still think that you're going to Heaven because of your faith in Christ—and depending on the interior state of your soul (which only God can see), you might be right. Great! I'm happy for you! But what about the rest of us—your brothers and sisters? What are you doing to help us? Jesus Christ said: "You will know them by their fruits" (Matt. 7:16). *By their fruits*, not by their faith alone. And to be fruitful, you have to do the things you're called to do as a Christian.

If you have any doubt about what I'm saying, go back and reread the parable of the sheep and the goats in Matthew 25. You'll see how crystal-clear and deadly serious Christ is about the necessity of *living your faith* by doing things to help your fellow human beings.

That's what we're talking about here: the kinds of things you're called to do as a Christian; the kinds of things that will bring you and the people closest to you peace and happiness—in this life and the next. And in order to do those things the right way, you need more than just a stretch of pretty sand! You need a map, my friend. You need a map!

Well guess what? You already have that map. We talked about it earlier in this book, but we didn't give it a name. It's called the *Holy Roman Catholic Church*!

You heard me. The Church. The very institution you may have left because it's too "organized."

"But isn't the Bible the map of Christianity?" you ask.

No, it's not. The Bible is the Word of God. It's the single most important book in the world.

It has the power to bestow life-changing grace on all who read it prayerfully. It tells the story of creation, redemption, and salvation. It tells the story of God's divine plan for angels and human beings. It tells the story of God's love for us, despite all our sins and shortcomings. It tells this incredible love story from its very beginning, showing how God's plan unfolded through time and how it will conclude at the end of time. As I said before, you need to read the Bible every day of your life. Remember: *no Bible, no breakfast; no Bible, no bed!*

But the Bible is not a map. The Bible is not even one book. It's a whole *library* of books, written and compiled at different times in history, for different audiences, and in different literary styles. Some books of the Bible are historical. Some books are allegorical. Some books are poetical. Some books are philosophical. Some books are theological. Some books are prophetic. Some books are practical wisdom and advice. Some books are songs. *All* the books of the Bible are inspired by God. But the Bible is not a simple, clear map of Christian living. It can't possibly serve that function because it's too varied in its content. It's too open to different interpretations. The Bible can be interpreted in fifty thousand ways. That's why there are fifty thousand Protestant denominations throughout the world and a million Protestant "popes."

So no, the Bible is not a map and was never meant to be. To accomplish *that* purpose, Jesus Christ founded His Church. The Church is the map of the Bible. The Church is the map of theology. The Church is the map of morality. The Church is the map of Christianity. The Church is the map of our personal relationship with God. The Church is the map of how to use our faith in the Lord. The Church is the map of how to be *fruitful* in the Kingdom of God.

The Church is the *map of life.*

As a map, the Church tells you the right way to go and the wrong way to go. It lays out all the pathways of grace in a neat and organized fashion. It gives you all the important landmarks and the distances between those landmarks. It tells you which way is up and which way is down. North, south, east, and west are all labeled clearly and correctly on this map. Moreover, it's a map that's understandable because it has a key—a key with symbols and icons and terms, all marked down and defined in a highly detailed manner.

In fact, not only is the Church a map, but it's the best kind of map—because it's a treasure map. Only on this map, the buried treasure isn't marked with an X but with a big *cross*.

This is what makes the phenomenon of people leaving the Church so mind-boggling. These well-meaning folks are looking so hard for their treasure. They want happiness. They want peace. They want certitude. They want meaning. They want purpose. They want Heaven. They want to love and help their neighbors. They want it all so badly that it makes them miserable. They spend their lives frantically searching for this treasure because they know it has got to be buried out there *somewhere*.

But instead of venturing out with their map to find it, all they do is walk up and down that same stretch of beach, repeating the same mindless mantra: "Organized religion is bad, organized religion is bad."

Have you ever seen those old beach bums on the shore, hunting for gold, trudging along the sand, waving a metal detector back and forth, searching for little bits of gold trinkets lost by other people? They hold their metal detectors in front of them like blind men clutching their walking sticks. Well, that's exactly what people who leave the Church are—blind men looking for gold on the beach! Yet all the while they have a beautiful, detailed, color-coded, treasure map right in their pocket—a map they don't want to use because it's too organized! A map they don't want to use because they think it's too difficult; because it tells them with too much clarity and accuracy and certitude how to find the buried treasure they're looking for. So they throw it away.

Amazing!

Now, does that mean these kinds of people can't locate any gold? Of course not. I'm not saying that Protestants or fallen-away Catholics can't find happiness in this life and Heaven in the next. They certainly can. A strong faith in God and love for the Lord can act like a spiritual GPS or homing device, guiding you to your destination, no matter how foggy your vision or muddled your thinking. In fact, these faith-filled people are probably a lot closer to the Kingdom of God than many of the hypocrites out there masquerading as Catholics. But that doesn't take away from the fact that Catholics who know their religion and try to sincerely practice it have a much *easier* time reaching their destination and finding their treasure.

Isn't that what you want too? Isn't that why you're reading this book? Because you're tired of wandering around without a purpose, making the same mistakes over and over? If so, then why don't you start using your map?

It's so simple. All you have to do is go out and get yourself a *catechism*. A catechism is nothing more than a summary of the principles of the Catholic religion—laid out in a very organized, systematic way. Essentially it's a "printout" of the map we've been talking about. It explains in easy-to-understand language all the main teachings and doctrines of the Faith, all the basic prayers, all the sacraments and sacramentals and devotions, all the pathways of grace. Along with reliable Catholic commentaries on the Old and New Testaments, it's a resource that can help guide you through the intricate labyrinth of biblical books, giving you sure and reliable interpretations of the most difficult scriptural passages, putting them into their proper context and theological perspective. In short, a catechism gives you all that is lacking in standard self-help programs as well as in other world religions and faith traditions. It gives you the *full* set of tools necessary to find happiness in this life and the next.

The "official" *Catechism of the Catholic Church* is very long—about nine hundred pages. If you're up to it, by all means go out and buy it and start reading it. But if you don't have the time, there are shorter, abbreviated versions that are excellent to use. The first one I ever read—right after I started wearing a cross (a story I related earlier)—was Fr. John Hardon's *Pocket Catholic Catechism*, and it changed my life. It's still available for purchase. But there are others, too, including the official *Compendium of the Catechism of the Catholic Church*, published by the United States Conference of Catholic Bishops, and the old original *Baltimore Catechism*, with versions for children and adults, as well as a revised St. Joseph's edition. These are all available digitally and in print—and are very cheap.

So do yourself a favor—get one right this second. It might be the single most important purchase you make in your lifetime.

Action Items

- ✓ Purchase any of the catechisms listed above, in either hard copy or for your tablet and smartphone. Then start reading it. You can go through it slowly, in the same way you're going through the Gospels. But begin right now, or immediately after you finish this thirty-day program.

The Time Machine

I read a good analogy once that applies to this discussion we're having. Interestingly, it wasn't in a spiritual book; it was in a weightlifting book. The writer was talking about how certain exercise machines had recently been invented that could help a person build muscle faster and more efficiently than standard barbells and dumbbells. But he was astonished that the weightlifting community didn't embrace this new technology. Instead, the experts seemed to actively fight against it. To illustrate his point, the writer told a story about a man digging in the ground for treasure. And this is where the analogy intersects with what we've been saying about finding the treasure marked by a big cross on the magnificent map given to us by the Church.

The writer said that once upon a time there was a man kneeling on the ground, digging into the dirt with both his hands. He was furiously burrowing away into the mud and soil and rocks to get under the surface. He was perspiring heavily and grunting and groaning, and his fingers were scratched and bloody from all the work he was doing. He was at it for hours and was able to uncover only a few inches of dirt. Then someone on horseback a short distance away noticed the man and rode up to him. He said, "My friend, I have no idea what you're doing, but I've got something that can help you," and with that he pulled out of his saddlebag a shovel and tried to hand it to the man. But then something very strange happened. Instead of accepting the gift with gratitude, the man on the ground became furious. His eyes turned red, and he shouted to the man on the horse, "Leave me alone!" Then he looked away in anger and continued digging frantically into the ground with his fingers.

Isn't that the very same thing we often experience when we try to help others? Don't they get mad at us? Don't they turn away indignantly and insist on continuing exactly what they were doing? Don't they "dig in" to their position with even more obstinance?

Well, I've got news for you. That's the same reaction so many people have when the Church reaches out to them with a helping hand, with a "shovel"; when she offers them the greatest personal-development tool in the world—the Catholic Mass.

Listen carefully to this—especially you fallen-away Catholics! In the story about the man on the ground digging with his hands, the ground represents the world; it represents all the difficulties of life; it represents all our problems; it represents the human mind; it represents our messed-up psychology. It's very hard to get through this ground, very hard to break through to the bottom of it. There are so many rocks and boulders and twisted roots you have to dig out before you can reach what you're looking for—for joy and purpose and transcendent peace and love and Heaven.

Well, God understands that. That's why the Church He founded doesn't give us only a map; it gives us the very tool we need to dig out our treasure. That's why on the night before He died, Christ instituted the Sacrament of His Body and Blood; that's why He gave us the Mass.

"Oh, but I don't get anything out of the Mass," you say.

You don't get anything out of the Mass? Putting aside for a moment the obvious response to this question—that you have an *obligation* to worship God because He gave you life, whether or not you "get anything out of" that worship—let's talk about this problem.

Fulton Sheen said that the reason many people don't get anything out of the Mass is that they don't bring anything *to* the Mass. If you've never played or watched football in your life, and have no idea what the objective of the game is or what the rules are, then you can't very well be expected to plop down in front of a TV on a Sunday afternoon and "get anything out of" the game everyone else is so excited about, can you? Or if you attend an opera, and haven't read the libretto beforehand, and don't understand the story or the words, and haven't accustomed yourself to that particular style of music (so different from what you normally listen to), how in the world can you possibly appreciate what so many others consider sublime and even glorious?

Yes, it's true that you can understand football and still dislike it, and you can understand opera and still dislike it. But *without* understanding these things, you have no chance at all of "getting anything out of" them.

It's the same with the Mass. Sure, people know that the Mass—like every other Christian worship service—centers on Jesus Christ and His teachings, and especially on the fact that He died on a Cross and rose from the dead so that we could have our sins forgiven and experience life everlasting in Heaven. That's all good and true. But what most people don't understand—including most Catholics—is that the Mass is a *time machine*. Literally and truly, a time machine!

I'm not speaking in figurative language here. A form of mystical time travel takes place at every single Catholic Mass. Only the Mass doesn't transport us back in time to the moment when Christ was crucified; it transports the moment of the Crucifixion forward in time to us—so that we can experience that monumental, life-saving event in our present-day lives.

That's why the priest wears strange, long, flowing vestments—so that he might resemble Jesus, who also wore a long, flowing robe. That's why the priest must climb several steps to the altar—to remind people of the hill named Calvary on which Christ was crucified. Every part of the Mass means something. Every detail has been carefully chosen to help worshippers understand that when the doors of that church close and the priest starts walking down the center or side aisle to the altar, the place in which they are standing is no longer simply another building, no longer simply another Christian church or religious temple. It is a special chamber built for spiritual time travel.

During the Mass, at the moment of consecration, the Cross and the Crucifixion are brought from the past and planted right there in the church, on that symbol of Calvary, the altar. Though they are invisible to the eye, the same Crucifixion that took place two thousand years ago and the very same Jesus Christ who was killed two thousand years ago are present in front of you. Remember, Christians believe that Jesus is God. Yes, Jesus was also a man, and as a man, He lived and walked in ancient Palestine. But as God, He stands outside time and space. As God, He is not bound by the rules of the clock. He is not bound by the rules of geography. During the Mass—in some miraculous way we can never fully understand this side of Heaven—the eternal God-Man "transports" Himself at the exact moment He sacrificed Himself on the Cross, to this very moment, *now*.

Let me put it another way.

If you lived two thousand years ago and stood among the Israelites and Romans that sad and tragic Friday afternoon that we now call "Good," you would have seen Jesus Christ killed. But if, at the moment of His death, you closed your eyes and covered your ears with your hands to block out all the extraneous details, you would have had *the same exact experience* that a Catholic has at Mass every Sunday. Likewise, if you attend Mass on a Sunday morning, and close your eyes and cover your ears at the moment the priest says the words, "This is my Body, which is given up for you" and holds the Host above his head, you will be experiencing *the very same Crucifixion* that occurred on Calvary two thousand years ago.

It won't look the same. It won't sound the same. It won't be brutal and bloody and agonizing. But it nevertheless *is* the same. The apostle John, standing under the Cross when his Master died, did not have *more* of an experience of the Crucifixion than an average Catholic Mass-goer. And an average Catholic Mass-goer does not have *less* of an experience of the Crucifixion than the apostle John. The Crucifixion was *equally* present to both of them—despite appearances. As Catholics, we believe God has the power to do that.

The *Catechism of the Catholic Church* (CCC) teaches clearly in paragraph 1323: Jesus instituted the Mass "in order to perpetuate the sacrifice of the cross throughout the ages until he should come again."

Are you getting it yet? The Mass is not a "replay" of a historical event. Nor is it Jesus Christ's sacrifice somehow repeated. Jesus died only *once*. He sacrificed His life for us only *once*. The Mass is not a do-over. It's the *same* Crucifixion. The *same* sacrifice. The *same* Jesus—now acting in the person of the priest. That once-and-forever sacrifice has been mystically transported across the millennia, by the time machine known as the Holy Sacrifice of the Mass. That's why it doesn't matter so much to faithful Catholics if the singing at Mass is bad, or if the preaching is boring, or if the interior of the church is ugly. They're not there for any of that. They're there to be present at the Crucifixion.

Now why would anyone want to be present at the Crucifixion? It would take a whole book to explain adequately, but here's the main idea in a nutshell: Catholics want to be present at the Crucifixion of Christ so that they can also experience the *Resurrection* of Christ.

Listen, everyone in life is carrying some kind of cross, right? Don't you have a cross? Don't you have many crosses? Maybe you've got some major health problems. Maybe you've got some serious financial challenges. Maybe you're very insecure or shy or lonely or depressed. Maybe you have a terrible temper. Maybe your libido is out of control. Maybe you've done some bad things that are causing you tremendous guilt. Maybe you've even confessed your sins and been forgiven, but the guilt still won't go away. Maybe your body is your cross. Maybe your job is your cross. Maybe your marriage is your cross. Maybe your kids are your cross. Maybe your whole life is your cross!

When Catholics go to Mass, we bring our crosses to the church with us. All those small and large crosses are in the church, in the pews beside us. At the moment of consecration, when the giant Cross of Christ is brought forward through time and planted on the altar in front of us, it's not alone in the church. It's surrounded by all our crosses, too. The next time you attend Mass, close your eyes and try to imagine that scene. On the altar is the Cross of the Lord, and surrounding it are all the smaller, individual crosses that belong to us. That's a true picture of the invisible reality of the Mass.

But what happened to Jesus Christ after He died on His Cross? He rose from the dead, didn't He? He rose in power and glory. He ascended into Heaven. That's the whole point of Christianity, isn't it? Well, the whole point of the Mass is that we get to join with Christ in what He did. We get to participate in His sacrifice in a profoundly meaningful and mystical way. We get to offer our own lives, our own problems, our own crosses to Him, and He, in turn, accepts that offering and joins our crosses to His, making it possible for us to experience rebirth and resurrection too—just as He did.

Do you see why the Mass is the greatest personal-development tool ever created? By virtue of this miraculous time machine, human beings are not only able to be present at the Crucifixion; we're able to plug into the power of the Resurrection, the power of new life, the power of Heaven. Do you think that might be something valuable to you as you try to overcome the problems of life?

But how, exactly, do you plug into this amazing power source? The answer is simple: by worthily receiving the sacrament of the Eucharist. Lots of Christian churches offer some form of "communion," but only the Catholic Church has the true Eucharist. Scott Hahn explains:

> At every Mass, we consume Jesus's resurrected, glorified body under the appearance of bread and wine. We eat the flesh and drink the blood of the God who became man, died, and rose again. The body that we eat is the same body that hung on the cross, lay in the tomb, and then rose from the dead. That body is also the same body that passed through walls, that could be in Emmaus one minute and Jerusalem the next, and then ascended into heaven to sit at the right hand of the Father.[9]

The Catholic Church teaches that the Eucharist is really and truly God. It is *God made man*. It is the *Body, Blood, Soul, and Divinity*

[9] Scott Hahn, "The Eucharist and the Resurrection of the Body," St. Paul Center for Biblical Theology, April 29, 2020, https://stpaulcenter.com/the-eucharist-and-the-resurrection-of-the-body/.

of Jesus Christ. It's not a symbol. It's not pretend. It's not some pious practice. It's not some meaningless ritual. It's not just a recollection of past events. It is the Lord, miraculously present—and also miraculously *hidden*—under the appearances of bread and wine—i.e., the color, taste, feel, smell, and molecular structure of bread and wine.

That's why the miracle that happens at the moment of consecration is called *transubstantiation*—the transfer or conversion of the substance of bread and wine into the *substance* of the Body and Blood of Christ. If you've ever received Communion at a Catholic Mass, please understand that, in doing so, you have *never once* eaten bread or drunk wine. You have taken God into your body. It is God that you have consumed.

Now, why would you want to consume God? After all, isn't that strange? Isn't that weird? Doesn't it even sound creepy and cannibalistic?

It certainly might—until you understand the concept. In fact, one of the reasons the first Christians were persecuted was that a charge of cannibalism was leveled against them by the Romans. Early references from Justin Martyr and Tertullian make it abundantly clear that because of the Christian belief in the Real Presence of Jesus Christ in the Eucharist, Romans thought Christians were guilty of eating human flesh and blood.

But while it might sound bizarre to ignorant pagans and many present-day Protestants, anyone with some basic knowledge of theology or even a little medical common sense knows that the principle is quite logical.

Jesus Himself couldn't have been more clear. He said: "He who eats my flesh and drinks my blood abides in me, and I in him" (John 6:56). What Christ meant was that He gives Himself to us in the Eucharist as spiritual *nourishment*. By consuming His

Body and Blood, we become united to the person of Christ, and in being united to Christ, we are united not only to His humanity but also His *divinity*. Our mortal and corruptible natures are transformed by being joined to the source of all life—indeed to Life itself.

In everyday language, this translates into: *You are what you eat!*

Think about it. When you consume things that are bad for you, such as sugar and candy and fast food and junk food, your body is negatively affected, isn't it? Not only will you get heavy, but you'll start having all kinds of health problems. It's a simple fact that the worse you eat, the more your body deteriorates. In fact, it's not an exaggeration to say that if you eat garbage long enough, your body will turn into garbage.

The opposite is also true. If you drink lots of water and eat lots of vegetables and nutritious whole foods, chock-full of essential vitamins and minerals and antioxidants, your physiology is going to improve—not only on the outside, but on a cellular and molecular level.

Well, what do you think happens if you consume God? What do you think happens if you receive Communion on a regular basis, in a morally upright, worthy, faith-filled manner? You're going to become more like God. You're going to be lifted into a higher kind of life—a different way of life, a life that Christ described in the Gospels as "the Kingdom of Heaven." This is not only a life of increased virtue but a life of great power—power to follow the Golden Rule, power to love your enemies, power to bring peace wherever there is strife, power to accomplish things that seem absolutely impossible; a life characterized by humility, truth, beauty, goodness, and countless *miracles*; an immortal life that continues beyond the grave into eternity in Heaven. Most importantly, it is a life characterized by extraordinary closeness to God.

Protestants are always talking about the importance of having a "personal relationship" with the Lord. Well, what in the world can be more personal than taking the Lord into your body? Every time a Catholic worthily receives Communion, he takes the Body, Blood, Soul, and Divinity of Jesus Christ into his own body, blood, soul, and humanity!

Protestants are always saying we need to "invite Jesus into our hearts." Well, faithful Catholics don't just invite Jesus into their hearts; they invite Him into every atom of every cell of every capillary of every organ of their bodies. Talk about being open and welcoming! Talk about biblical hospitality! Every time you receive Communion, you're inviting Jesus into your truest home—the temple of your body.

I'll give you another way to look at it. Let's say you have a good friend who decides to move to the other side of the world, to a place you have no way of traveling to, for financial reasons or otherwise. Of course it's still possible to be friends with that person. You can call him on the phone, or you can send him letters or e-mails. But what if years go by and this friend never once visits you? What if you never see this friend in the flesh, or break bread with him, or shake his hand or hug him or speak to him in person? Yes, the friendship could endure. But how close could it really be? Wouldn't it be missing something? Something important?

That something is physical contact. You and I are human beings. We're not computers. We're not machines. We're not "graphical user interfaces." We're flesh-and-blood creatures that have immortal souls. We need to have personal *connection* for us to remain close to one another—not just text messages!

The same is true for our relationship with the Lord. Yes, we can pray to Him anytime we want. In fact, it's essential that we do that. God loves it when we pray to Him. And He's happy to speak to us and listen to us anytime, night or day. There are many people in the world who stay close to God by simply keeping up this regular, prayerful contact. But it's still sort of like making a phone call to Heaven.

God understands our need for something more. He understands our need for personal contact. He understands it because He created us. So while He encourages and even commands us to pray to Him, He also offers us something deeper. Even though He ascended into Heaven after His mission on earth was completed, He made it possible for people of every generation, through the Eucharist, to have a deeply personal, spiritual, and *physical* connection with Him as well.

That's closeness. *That's* intimacy. *That's* true personal relationship. And that's the kind of relationship every Catholic in the world can have with God because that's what the Eucharist is all about. The Eucharist is truly the "source and summit of the Christian life" because it contains "the whole spiritual good of the Church"—because it contains Christ Himself (CCC 1324).

Now, does this mean that if you receive the Eucharist once, it's going to magically turn you into a saint? Obviously not. We have plenty of evidence to the contrary, in the form of Catholics who go to Mass and then behave dismally. Sometimes that's because those particular Catholics are hypocrites; sometimes it's because they're not worthily receiving the sacrament; sometimes it's because they're very weak; sometimes it's because the devil is purposely attacking them *because* they've taken Jesus into their bodies.

Sometimes the reason is just that it takes *time* to become transformed. Again, we're human beings, and that means we have to filter everything—including God—through our physiology and psychology. The power of God is infinite, but we have only a finite ability to assimilate Him. It's something akin to being outdoors in the summer. Yes, the sun is tremendously powerful. Yes, it lights the whole solar system. Yes, it's bright and warm and life-sustaining. But when you step outside, you can't take in all that power at once. If you want to get a beautiful suntan or to use the sunlight to help your body manufacture vitamin D and keep you healthy, then you have to go outside regularly and consistently. You can't expect to take in all the sun's energy at once. It's the same with the Son of God. The power of a single consecrated Host is infinite. But neither you nor I nor anyone else has the power to absorb that power instantaneously. That's one of the reasons the Catholic Church has made it mandatory for Catholics to attend Mass every Sunday. It's because we need regular and consistent exposure to *the Son*—especially via the sacrament of the Eucharist.

Don't deprive yourself of that sacrament! Don't deprive yourself of the incredible treasure marked by a cross on the map we've been talking about throughout this book. If you're Protestant and love the Lord, I encourage you to do more research into the Catholic teaching on the Eucharist. I promise it will revolutionize your faith and bring you to an entirely new level of spirituality. And if you're a Catholic who has been away from the Church for a while—and if you really want to radically change your life for the better—I urge you to make a decision *now* to go to Confession and have your serious sins absolved by a validly ordained Catholic priest. Then, with the new understanding of the Liturgy that you've hopefully gained from this chapter, go to church, attend Mass, and at the proper time bow your head, make the Sign of the Cross, and humbly, respectfully, gratefully, prayerfully, faithfully, and worthily receive this most wondrous of all God's gifts to man.

Then let the Lord begin transforming you from the inside out.

Action Items

- ✓ This is the most important chapter in the entire book. Go back and read over the section on the Eucharist—even if you just finished it!
- ✓ Then, if you haven't been attending church, find out where the Mass is being celebrated near you, and go as soon as you can! If you haven't been to Confession in a while, by all means put it on your schedule to do so ASAP.
- ✓ If you attend Sunday Mass regularly, try going on one or two weekdays as well. Weekday Masses are usually shorter, and they're scheduled early in the morning so that people might attend them before going to work. In any case, the next time you're at Mass, close your eyes during the moment of consecration and try to imagine the Crucifixion, mystically "transported" across time to the present moment, with the Cross of Christ on the altar, and all the crosses of your fellow parishioners in the church surrounding you.
- ✓ If you're not yet a Catholic, try attending Mass at least once. Don't receive Holy Communion, but prayerfully observe all that goes on. Once the Mass is finished, if you have the inclination, tell the priest you're interested in exploring the Catholic Faith more. Ask him what your next step should be.

Immortal Combat

We've talked about a lot of topics so far, but do you want to know the truth? You can do everything this book has recommended and still end up being unhappy. That's right. You can set and achieve your goals; you can be grateful for all your blessings; you can believe in God and follow His commandments; you can repent and confess your sins whenever you fall; you can study the catechism every day; you can even go to church and practice your Faith and regularly receive Holy Communion—and yet you can still be a frustrated, confused human being.

Why? Because to really get a handle on things, there's something else you have to understand. There's something else you have to take into account as you make your way through the ups and downs of life. It's something the personal-development industry never talks about. In fact, it's something many Christians never talk about either. What is it?

It's called *evil.*

Yes, there is evil in the world. Not just unpleasant things. Not just problems. Not just setbacks. Not just "challenges." Not just "unproductive" ways of dealing with situations. There is evil—real, deadly, diabolical, black-as-night evil.

Self-help experts don't like to talk about that because they don't want to get anybody uncomfortable. They don't want to be viewed as "religious fanatics." They want to appeal to as many people as possible—even those who have completely lost faith in God. So they just don't mention the word "evil."

But there's a problem with not mentioning it. Even if you ignore evil, it's not going away. And that's why most of these personal-development techniques ultimately break down. You can listen to self-help audios and podcasts all the time and become well versed in the power of positive thinking and make good progress on achieving your goals and believing in yourself—and then one day, when you're least expecting it, evil strikes. Maybe someone you know is raped. Maybe an elderly couple in your neighborhood is brutally attacked. Maybe a little child from the local school is abducted, abused, and murdered by some deviant monster. Evil crimes occur all the time. And when they do, it's pretty hard to focus on the positive. It's pretty hard to believe that your "thoughts" control reality and that all that's required to "overcome challenges" is to manifest some kind of "positive energy" or "karma." All those easy catchphrases seem so empty in the light of hard, cold, merciless malevolence.

The truth is that you can ignore evil all you want, but evil is not going to ignore you. St. Paul said that our struggle in life is not with "flesh and blood" or even the rulers of this world, but rather with "powers and principalities" (see Eph. 6:12). Do you know what "powers and principalities" are? Those are specific kinds of angels—in this case, fallen angels (better known as demons) and their leader, the devil.

Now, many people in our enlightened culture scoff at the idea of the devil and dismiss any notion of a spiritual world beyond the senses. But if you call yourself a Christian, you're still supposed to believe in those invisible realities. And the reason you're supposed to believe in them is that they're true—they do exist, and they do try to influence people to do bad things.

Like it or not, believe it or not, there's a real spiritual war going on. If you need evidence, just look inside yourself. Look at your own inner battles—all the temptations you have to face on a daily basis—all your dark secrets, all your lusts, all your jealousies, all your grudges, all the little pleasures you sometimes feel when bad things happen to other people. Then look around you. Look at all the terrible evil in the news—the crimes, the drugs, the rapes, the murders, the tortures, the acts of terrorism, the child molestations, the child pornography, the sadistic violence. Look at the "big" societal evils—the murder rates, the suicide rates, the wars, the genocides. Just look at the abortion rate—twenty million babies killed a year, worldwide. A veritable ocean of blood!

Please don't misunderstand me. I'm not calling anyone in particular evil. Take abortion as an example. God knows that most women who have abortions do so because they feel trapped and pressured by their circumstances and by their families and by their boyfriends. They don't have abortions because of "freedom of choice" but rather because they feel they have *no freedom* and *no choice*. Of course God has mercy on them. Of course God wants to forgive them. As I've already said in this book, anyone can be forgiven for any sin—no matter how bad—as long as he or she is truly sorry. One tiny drop of Christ's blood is enough to wash away the sins of a billion universes.

But a sin can't be forgiven if you don't think it's a sin. An evil can't be washed away if you insist that it's really a good. In theology, that's what's called a "diabolical inversion." It's when the truth becomes a lie, and a lie becomes the truth. It's what the "powers and principalities" St. Paul spoke of are always working to accomplish. They want a world in which morality is upside down, in which the positive is negative and the negative is positive.

But let me ask you a question: What happens in life when you do that? What happens when you reverse the polarities of an electric current, for instance—when you switch the charges and make the negative positive? What happens if you do that with the electric wiring in your home? The power gets cut! The lights go out! Darkness envelops everything.

And isn't that exactly the state of our society today? Isn't that exactly the state of so many people's lives? Hasn't the whole moral system been turned on its head? Men claim that they're women, and women claim that they're men. Promiscuity is viewed as empowering, while chastity is dismissed as insanity. Unborn babies with hearts that beat, lungs that breathe, and nerves that feel are called blobs of tissue with fewer rights than sea turtles. The elderly and infirm aren't treated as the wisest, most treasured members of society but rather are killed because they're in the way. Innocent children are given transgender indoctrination in grammar school but are not allowed to pray to God. They're also legally permitted to get abortions and sex-change operations while adults who object are branded as "anti-child," "anti-choice," "religious fanatics," and "homophobic."

Hasn't black become white and white become black? Aren't we literally entrenched in a culture of atheistic deceit, despair, relativism, and death? Doesn't spiritual darkness prevail everywhere?

That's one of the main reasons there's so much unhappiness in the world—why there's so much stress, fear, desolation, emptiness, loneliness, and hopelessness. In the twenty-first century, despite all our economic prosperity and technological and medical advances, we are a world mired in moral misery.

And it's very understandable. When darkness prevails on such a large scale, it's almost impossible to be happy—and it doesn't matter what kind of self-help techniques you employ.

The sins that afflict modern society and that afflict each of us personally are not just psychological or physical in nature. If they were, we would need only psychological or physical weapons to combat them. But there's a large spiritual component involved. The temptations we face—to pride, promiscuity, gluttony, laziness, anger, cruelty, envy, selfishness, infidelity, despair, untruthfulness, disobedience to God, unwillingness to repent, and so on—are very real and very strong. And they never let up. Sometimes they seem to take a rest, but not for long. They're always there, trying to act on us in a negative way, trying to pull us down into the slimy gutter—heavy, powerful, and relentless.

Now, of course, the best thing to do is strengthen your will to such a degree that you can resist these strong temptations. As I said in a book I wrote on the subject of Hell, the devil is like a vicious dog on a six-foot chain. The most effective counterstrategy to all his terrible attacks can be summed up in five little words: *don't get in his range!*

If you want to avoid being trapped in the jaws of the evil one, you can't get too close to him. It's that simple. And the best way to do that is to stop committing serious sins. Sinning—and in particular, obstinate sinning—is the equivalent of running away from God and into the devil's arms. If you stay far enough away from the devil, all he can do is bark and try to frighten you. He's just another harmless dog on a chain. The only way he can hurt you is if you give yourself to him.

So don't!

But if, despite your best efforts, you find yourself in the devil's clutches, don't make the mistake of thinking you can fight him off the same way you do the other annoying problems in your life. Don't think that the self-help industry can rescue you—because it can't.

Personal-development tools are wonderful for giving us confidence and teaching us ways to schedule our time and achieve our goals, but in the end, they're just not effective at preventing these kinds of temptations from wreaking havoc in our lives. And the reason is that *you can't fight a spiritual battle with worldly weapons.* When you try to do that, the "powers and principalities" sit back and laugh at you! They know that you need to use spiritual weapons for that kind of combat—otherwise, you get nowhere.

Christ Himself said that certain "demons" could be overcome only by "prayer and fasting" (Mark 9:29). He didn't say they could be overcome with positive thinking or with affirmations or with written goals or with the help of support groups or even with normal religious practices—beneficial as those things may be. He said that certain spiritual enemies were so powerful and tenacious they could be driven out *only* by prayer and fasting. And if Christ said it, you can be sure it's true.

So let me ask you a question: Do you pray and fast? If not, then you shouldn't complain that you have temptations that are too difficult to resist. The fact is, you're not taking advantage of two of the most important spiritual weapons God gave you to fight evil. Of course you're having trouble with lying or with lust or with rage or with laziness. Of course you're on the wrong side of the issue when it comes to abortion or euthanasia or sex-change operations. It makes perfect sense that you can't make progress in either overcoming "hard" sins or obtaining clarity about the difference between good and evil in the world.

I said earlier that you should pray when you wake up in the morning and before you go to bed at night. And that's very true.

But if you've got serious problems in your life, you need to pray a lot more than that. You need to continually raise your mind to God throughout the day. You need to regularly take the time to find a quiet place and focus on God. When you start focusing more on God, He'll start focusing even more on you and on your problems. Yes, it's true that God is always thinking about you, even when you're not thinking about Him. Yes, it's true that God loves everyone and wants everyone to go to Heaven. But God does favors for His friends. He gives the most assistance to those who are closest to Him. And the best way to get close to God is to talk to Him as much as possible.

For goodness' sake, don't be afraid of being branded a "religious fanatic." You should be doing everything you can to be on intimate terms with God. You should be prayerfully reading the Bible every day. You should be studying that catechism. You should be praying novenas. You should be enlisting the help of the saints. You should be enlisting the help of the angels. You should be praying the Rosary and the Chaplet of Divine Mercy and the Angelus and even the Liturgy of the Hours. You should be going to Confession frequently. You should be making use of sacramentals, such as the scapular and the Miraculous Medal and the crucifix and holy water. You should be going to Eucharistic adoration and spending time before the Blessed Sacrament. Most importantly, you should be attending Mass—if possible, every day—and receiving the Body, Blood, Soul, and Divinity of Christ. All of these are extremely powerful forms of prayer; all can help you take your personal relationship with the Lord to a new level, and all of them—together—are needed during times of great moral crisis.

If you're under *serious and prolonged* attack from the devil, there's one other devotion I'd like to recommend, especially to those of you who are committed Catholics and love your Faith. It's not within the scope of this book to discuss it at length, but when it comes to fighting evil, it's the equivalent of using the nuclear option. It's called Consecration to Jesus through Mary. Essentially, it's asking Jesus to come into your life and transform it in the same way He chose to come into the world: through the Blessed Virgin Mary—whom Catholics believe to be the spouse of the Holy Spirt (Luke 1:35). Do some research on the traditional method of making this consecration, according to St. Louis de Montfort, and the excellent newer version by Fr. Michael Gaitley. Again, we don't have time to go over this practice now, and it's something that's very misunderstood—especially by Protestants—but take my word, it will revolutionize your life.

And by the way, even if you're Protestant and don't believe in the value of any of these prayers and devotions, you *still* have to attend your own church regularly. Why? Because if you don't, you're missing out on one of the most incredible spiritual weapons that God has given to you to fight evil. To be a Christian means that you're part of a family. When Jesus taught us to pray, He didn't tell us to say "My Father, who art in Heaven"; He told us to say "*Our* Father." He also said to His disciples, "When *two or three* gather together in my name—I shall be there among them" (see Matt. 18:20).

Believing in God is not strictly a one-on-one affair. It involves everyone. It involves the whole community of believers. Having a personal relationship with the Lord—which is something everyone needs—is never an excuse for self-absorption, self-centeredness, and isolation. As we noted earlier in this book, it's no accident that the symbol of our Faith isn't a circle or some other closed figure but, rather, a cross, with its beams extending outward in all directions—to all four corners of the globe and even beyond that, into the next world. To be a Christian, by definition, means to go *out* of yourself and not just to retreat inward.

Then there's fasting. Everyone forgets about fasting, and yet it's absolutely essential to your spiritual life. We talked about this earlier. Fasting is when you willingly refrain from doing something that's morally permissible because you want to make a sacrifice for God. Usually, people refrain from eating for a period of time. And that's probably the best kind of fasting because it directly affects your body. But as I've said, you can fast from anything: music, social media, television, e-mail, shopping—whatever you really enjoy doing. The key is that it's got to be *difficult*. You can't give up something that's easy for you. The whole point is to feel "hungry" and to resist *giving in* to that hunger.

There's just no end to the spiritual benefits of fasting. It breaks the pattern and routine of your daily activities—activities that are sometimes conducive to sinning. It "resets" your entire system. It disciplines your will. It disciplines your flesh. It strengthens them both far beyond their normal capacity. It purifies your body and spirit and makes it possible for you to pray much more deeply and resist temptation much more easily. It makes it possible for you to appreciate all the blessings you have and to fight harder to keep them. Remember, all the Old Testament prophets prayed and fasted. Jesus prayed and fasted. His disciples prayed and fasted. The early Church prayed and fasted. And great Christians down through the ages have prayed and fasted. There's a reason they did it: *it works*. And if it worked for them, it can work for you.

Yes, people rarely try it. Then they complain that Christian morality is too difficult to practice.

Too difficult to practice? Of course it's too difficult to practice! In fact, it's impossible to practice the way most Christians go about it. How in the world can you hope to follow the moral teaching of

Jesus Christ in this secular, hedonistic, morally upside-down age without ever getting any spiritual nourishment from Jesus Christ? And how can you even think of mustering enough courage to take part in the great spiritual culture war that's raging all around us when you don't even have the most rudimentary spiritual weapons at your disposal? It's like trying to defeat an enemy when you're naked and have both hands tied behind your back. To quote Chesterton again, "The Christian ideal has not been tried and found wanting. It has been found difficult; and left untried."[10]

St. Paul said it a different way. In a famous passage from his Letter to the Ephesians, he warned believers about the need to "put on the full armor of God, so that when the day of evil comes, you may be able to stand your ground" (6:13, NIV).

Notice that he said the *full* armor of God. Not some of the armor. Not a piece of the armor. But all of it. Every last bit of it. The reason he said that is that the devil is a good shot! If you have big holes in your defenses, you're going to get hit—and you're going to fall.

Don't make that mistake! Don't spend decades amassing money and friends and reputation and power and personal-development skills in an attempt to secure happiness, and then forget that evil can wipe it all out in the blink of an eye. Don't be so naïve to think you're safe and secure—because you're not. Nobody is. Instead, be intelligent—spiritually intelligent. Find some good books on spiritual combat and study them. Pray and fast regularly, especially during times of great temptation. Read the Bible, not just once in a while, but every day. Worship and receive the sacraments with your fellow believers; don't be arrogant and try to do it by yourself.

[10] G. K. Chesterton, *What's Wrong with the World* (Manchester, NH: Sophia Institute Press, 2021), 31.

Above all, learn your faith, increase your faith, and be sure that God is the center of your life.

If you use these and other spiritual weapons, then, when that day of evil comes, you'll be able to stand your ground without wavering, just as St. Paul promised. You'll be able to be happy even in the midst of the worst trials. Indeed, you'll be able to *overcome* the worst trials. And if you persevere in using these weapons, I guarantee that no matter how deep the darkness that surrounds you, your light will always shine forth and serve as a powerful beacon to your family and your friends and all who know you.

That's a heck of a lot more than any kind of positive thinking will ever do for you.

Action Items

- ✓ Make a battle plan for resisting spiritual evil when it comes your way. Pick at least five types of prayer you intend to use when this day of trial comes. Pick at least five favorite foods and/or activities that you intend to fast from as well. Write them all down under the heading "My Spiritual Weapons."

Intense Suffering

Yesterday, we talked about evil. Today, we're going to talk about suffering. I know it's not a lot of fun reading about these subjects. Believe me, it's even less fun writing about them. But I want this book to give you a whole program for life, and in order to do that, I have to include those things that make life so hard and so painful so much of the time.

I also want to be fair. I've taken a few shots at the personal-development industry in this book, but when it comes to dealing with much of the frustration and depression we experience on a daily basis, self-help programs can be quite effective. For example, I've learned some important things from the work of Tony Robbins—things that have helped shape who I am and inspired me to get back on track when I've been in a rut; things that have shown me how to stay positive when I've felt overwhelmed by problems.

It's not always easy to do that. The human brain always seems to gravitate to the negative. In fact, I know a lot of people who specialize in being pessimistic. You meet them for breakfast or lunch, and within five minutes, they've complained about everything from the slow service of the waiters to the lighting in the room to the problems in the Middle East. Do you know any people like that? They're pretty hard to deal with, aren't they? They just zero in like laser beams on everything that's wrong with the world. Their focus is always negative, and they wonder why they're miserable!

The self-help industry helped me realize the importance of disciplining my thinking so I could more easily focus on the positive—even when I was feeling negative. Being a full-blooded Italian and passionate by nature, I find that it's never very difficult for my "temperature" to rise. And as I've already said, living in New York City has not exactly been a calming influence. When stressful situations occur, it's easy to slip into a foul, complaining, self-pitying mode. It's easy to say things like "Why does this always happen to me?"

But by constant practice and self-discipline, I've tried to learn to make the most of stressful situations by asking myself questions like "What can I learn from this problem?" or "What can I do now that will give me some hope?" or "Despite this challenge, what am I grateful for?" or "What new level is God trying to take me to by giving me this suffering?" I've discovered that it's much simpler to be happy when you're able to control your thinking process; when you're able to train your mind to resist the pull of emotional gravity; when you're able to finally break the habit of negative thinking.

I've also learned to spend no more than 10 percent of my time thinking about my problems. The other 90 percent has to be devoted to trying to figure out their solutions. Usually people do the reverse, don't they? They dwell too much on the details of their problems. They play the "tape" of their troubles over and over again in their minds until they work themselves up into a state of black depression. And once they're in that state, it's hard for them to get out of it. Usually, they end up taking the easy route of *temporarily* relieving their pain by doing things that aren't always good for them—physically, mentally, or spiritually. What they don't realize is that it's a lot more effective to spend your time fixing your problems instead of fixating on them. Yes, it takes a certain kind of mental discipline to do that, but it's possible—and the self-help industry is good at teaching it.

But then there are problems that no personal-development technique in the world can remedy. And this is where Christianity comes into play again because Christianity teaches that while it's possible to be joyful under any circumstances, life on this earth will always be a valley of tears and a place of trial. To deny that is to deny reality itself. To live is to suffer—sometimes, to suffer intensely. And when intense suffering comes—whether it's grieving over the loss of someone you love, or the fear of that kind of loss—there's only one thing that really works: *total abandonment to the will of God.*

What you have to understand is that nothing happens in the universe unless God either wills it or allows it to happen. Nothing happens to *you* unless God wills it or allows it to happen. Nothing in life occurs by chance; nothing is an accident; nothing is a coincidence.

That doesn't mean that God *wants* tragic things—like car accidents and diseases and terrorist attacks and worldwide pandemics—to take place. God isn't some sadistic witch doctor poking pins in His human puppets in order to cause them pain. He would much rather that our lives be free from suffering. But the fact is, He has chosen to create a world in which free will prevails—a world in which evil and suffering can occur. Believe it or not, that kind of world is actually better. It actually makes a deeper, more profound kind of happiness possible because it's predicated on freedom and not on automation. After all, computers and robots and smartphones and anything that's programmed can't be happy, right? Basically, God permits evil only because He knows that someday, some way, by the mysterious workings of His divine providence,

He's going to pull some greater good out of it. And some greater good out of *you*.

What possible "greater good" might come out of your suffering?

Maybe your problem will bring you closer to God. After all, dependence on God equals intimacy with God.

Or maybe this is a chance for you to help others who have the same problem.

Or maybe this is an opportunity for you to *receive* help from other people.

Who knows? All I can say for sure is that whenever God allows you to undergo a period of trial and suffering, He's trying to purify you; He's trying to "prune the vine." And the goal of every purification and every pruning is always the same: to produce more fruit. God wants you to produce more fruit for Him and more fruit for His Kingdom. And though you may not realize it at the moment you're experiencing pain, more fruit always means more *life*. When God gives you suffering, He is actually giving you the opportunity to do more and to grow more and to love more and therefore to *live* more.

That's why you have to accept on faith that everything in life—whether it's wealth, poverty, sickness, health, blessings, or trials—comes from the hand of God and ultimately is for the benefit of your immortal soul.

Now, it's important to be careful here. Abandonment to God's will isn't to be confused with fatalism or quietism or cowardice. Just because God is in charge doesn't mean that you sit back and do nothing when action is called for. Quite the contrary. If a problem arises, you have to deal with it. If you're sick, you have to call a doctor. If you're in legal trouble, you have to call a lawyer. If you see an injustice, you have to fight it. God expects you to do everything that needs to be done in order to solve your problem. But once you're finished, you have to let it go. You have to relinquish it. You have to try your best to be at peace—to know in the deepest part of your soul that God is in control. If, despite your best efforts, all your hopes and dreams seem to be dashed, you have to accept that as part of God's plan for you.

Is that always easy to do? Of course not! As I've said so often in this book, it's sometimes impossible to control your feelings, even on an hour-to-hour basis. But abandonment isn't about feelings. It's about your will. When you see yourself worrying about a problem, when you see the anxiety and fear starting to build inside you, that's the time to make a conscious effort to take a breath, recollect yourself, and say with confidence, "I know You're here with me, God. I know You're watching over me. I know this is Your will. I know that nothing happens without Your permission." So while your emotions may revolt and even tremble, your will can still be at peace and say, "No, I will not be afraid."

Let's be honest. Everyone's life is in question every day. There is absolutely no certainty about life or death. At any moment, you can have a heart attack or a brain aneurysm; you can be in a car accident or get hit by a bus. Once again—the same God who gave you the morning does not promise you the evening. Each day is truly and literally a gift. Whenever God allows you or someone you know to get a serious illness or face any kind of serious problem, He wants to make that point clear. He wants to drive home the fact that everyone's life is in His hands, that everyone must literally depend on Him for every breath they take.

That includes *you*. Do you understand that? You have to stop taking that for granted!

All that we know for sure—the only certainty we *do* have—is that while we're here and living, we have the ability to love, serve, and help the people around us; and to increase *their* faith, love, and trust in God.

Think of all the things that could have gone wrong when you were conceived—before you were even born; think of all the things that have gone wrong in your life up till now. Think of all the situations God has brought you through safely. Think of all that He has arranged and taken care of in your life. Think of all the big prayers He has answered. Well, the same God who cared for you throughout your life is going to take care of you today, tomorrow, and every other day. Either He will shield you from suffering, or He will give you the strength to bear it.

Listen, the devil delights in your fear and anxiety. Remember that! Anxiety is the greatest spiritual enemy, after sin. It has been said that God commands you to pray, but He forbids you to worry. Why? Because anxiety incapacitates you. It paralyzes you. It stops you from following God's will. It stops you from helping others and loving others. It stops you from sacrificing. It stops all goodness and leaves a void in which the devil has space to operate to the maximum extent. There's an old saying: "The devil fishes in troubled waters." You must not allow him to do that! Yes, on the surface, the waters of your soul can be stirred, but deeper underneath you must be at peace.

Of course, that's hard to do. In fact, there may be times when it seems impossible for you to be at peace; times when you're deathly afraid that something terrible might happen, such as financial ruin, or the breakup of your marriage, or cancer; times when you literally find it difficult to breathe, when your whole body goes limp, when your knees start to buckle and the only thing you want to do is collapse somewhere—anywhere—and close your eyes and shut out the whole world.

In those dark days of radical fear, radical abandonment is the only answer. Christ said in one translation of the Gospels, "Fear is useless; what is needed is trust" (see Mark 5:36). When He said that, He was speaking as God Almighty, and He was speaking for all times and for all situations.

The simple fact is that the more you trust God, the more He'll help you get through whatever crisis you're experiencing. He may not perform any miracles for you or take away the crisis itself, but He'll always get you through the storm with your faith and peace of mind intact. No matter how great your fear, you just have to keep saying, "Jesus, I trust in You; Jesus, I trust in You." It doesn't matter if you say it a million times. You just have to say it over and over again, out loud and to yourself, morning, noon, and night, as you drift off to sleep and as you wake up. You have to make it part of your very breathing.

Now what does "trusting Jesus" mean, in practical terms? I'll tell you. It means going about your daily work without thinking about the problem you have left in Jesus' hands. If you have a job, and you're physically able, you should keep on working. If there are meetings you have to attend, attend them. If you have projects you have to complete, complete them. If there's a certain exercise routine you're supposed to follow, follow it. In other words, the way you show God that you trust Him is by not letting your problems consume all your thoughts and emotions and activities. Essentially, you show your trust in God by forcing yourself not to think about your problems but instead, letting Him think about them!

Do you know one way that you can continually pray to God about your problem without fixating on it? There's a very short and effective prayer you can say without actually saying a word. It's called *the Sign of the Cross*. People forget that this is a prayer, but it is! By making the Sign of the Cross, you're physically branding yourself with the very instrument that Christ used to save the world. You're showing faith in the Cross of Christ, in Christ crucified, and in Christ risen from the dead. That's powerful! If you're going through a period of great stress or suffering, you should make the Sign of the Cross dozens of times a day. You don't have to say a single word or think a single thought. You're demonstrating your trust in God by praying with your body. Each time you make the Sign of the Cross, you're sending an SOS signal up to God. Believe me, that's something God is going to notice.

Another important point to keep in mind has to do with *timing*. Christ said, "Do not be anxious about tomorrow, for tomorrow will be anxious for itself. Let the day's own trouble be sufficient for the day" (Matt. 6:34). What that means is that God gives you divine assistance, or "grace," only for the present day; and He dispenses that grace only one day at a time. He doesn't give you grace for tomorrow, or for next week or for next month. Just for this one twenty-four-hour period. That's why the fear of some future suffering is always greater than the suffering itself. When you're thinking about painful events that might take place tomorrow, you are not yet being given the grace God intends to give you *at the moment* you'll be experiencing those events tomorrow. This is a key point to grasp. The pain you have now anticipating your suffering is greater than the actual suffering will be, because right now you're not being given any divine help to deal with that suffering. You're only being given help to get through the day.

What that means is that when you undergo any kind of great fear and anxiety, one of the most important things you must do is *shorten your time frame*. You need to focus specifically and exclusively on the one day that you're presently living. You can't keep repeating all the various nightmare scenarios in your head. You can't think about the financial ruin you might experience next week, or the scandal you might be involved in two weeks from now, or the cancer that might possibly spread next month, or the complications that might occur during surgery in two months, or the person you love dying next year. All that worrying about future disasters is useless. More importantly, it's an obstacle to receiving divine help from God.

Yes, an obstacle. God wants you to trust Him. And thinking about all those terrible things that aren't even necessarily going to happen is not a sign of trust. It's a sign of presumption and despair and faithlessness. God is interested in giving you divine assistance only today and only if you trust Him. If you welcome that assistance, He is going to help you *solve* your problems tomorrow.

For goodness' sake, don't doubt that! Don't doubt the power of God to help you! Don't doubt God's desire to help you!

Therefore, your goal is not to think about the coming days and weeks and months. Your goal is to get through the day. You *must* get through the day and make it to nighttime. That's your main objective in life whenever you experience crippling anxiety. And when you finally get to bed, sleep is your reward. Don't underestimate the power of sleep. Sleep is powerful. Sleep is your friend. Two things happen when you sleep. One is spiritual. The Bible says that God pours out His blessings on those He loves when they slumber (see Ps. 127:2); that's because they are trusting Him with their problems. The other is physical. The body does all its internal repair work at night. All your systems go into a "sleep mode" and actually work on fixing themselves. So if you're experiencing profound stress, your objective is always to get a good night's sleep.

If you need help, don't hesitate to buy an over-the-counter sleep aid or ask your doctor to prescribe something stronger. Listen, it's neither silly nor cowardly to knock yourself out if you have to! Do whatever is necessary at night to sleep soundly. Your bedroom should be a safe haven for you, not a torture chamber of horrors. Once you're there—once you've made it through the day, you have to be able to put your troubles aside. You have to be able to place whatever "cross" God has given you in the corner, against the wall; then climb into bed, give all your anxiety to God, go to sleep, and let *Him* work on your problems for the next eight hours—as well as let your body heal itself and build up your energy reserves so you can do all you need to do the *following* day.

Don't worry about your cross—it'll still be there when you get up.

Here's one last practical idea. Like some of my Evangelical friends, I have a folder in my desk drawer labeled "Problems for God." When I have something to deal with that's outside my immediate control—or something that's too big for me to handle—I put it down in this file. I literally tell God, "This is Your problem, God; please take care of it for me." You should do the same thing. Create a list like this, keep it in a folder, and put a heavy wooden cross right on top of it. You can do this in a computer file too, but it's much better to use a physical folder—that way, you can see and touch and handle and *close* it.

My friend, if you're going through a serious problem, I assure you that you have the power to do this. St. Paul said, "Dismiss all anxiety from your mind" (see Phil. 4:6). That wasn't a suggestion of his. It was a command from God. And God would not command us to do something unless He also gave us the power to follow that command. Think of a judge in a courtroom. When he slams the gavel down in front of him, it means no more questions, no more witnesses, no more cross-examinations, case *dismissed*! That's what you have to do when you find that your mind keeps coming back and circling around the same fearful thoughts. You must bang the gavel down and say, "*Enough*, *stop*, case *dismissed*!

Now, if someone close to you has already died, you might have to do a few other things as well to make it through the searing pain.

Not only do you have to trust that God has a plan for you, but you also have to trust that God has a plan for the person who died. You have to trust that God took that person at exactly the right moment, at the moment that was best *for that person's immortal soul.*

You have to trust that time really does heal all wounds. It may take years, but the pain *will* eventually subside. At the very least, it will be dulled. The important thing to understand is that people heal in their own ways and at their own rates. Don't ever let anyone tell you differently. If some well-meaning friends think you've been grieving too long and that it's time to "move on," then it's time to politely tell *them* to move on—to some other place or some other topic of conversation.

Then there's that old saying about the healing power of salt. Have you ever heard it? "Salt is the remedy for all grieving." Not table salt, of course. But salt from the sweat of hard work, salt from the tears of crying, and salt that comes from being near or on the sea. Those three things always seem to act as a soothing balm for the wounded soul. Try them.

And finally, if none of that works, you can try one other remedy for grieving the loss of someone: you can try thinking long and hard about a place called Heaven. People today just don't think about Heaven enough. I've written an adult book and two children's books on the subject because I don't believe there's anything more important in the spiritual life to pray about or meditate on. If people meditated on Heaven for five minutes a day, their lives would be completely transformed.

The Bible says that "eye has not seen, nor ear heard, nor have entered into the heart of man, the things that God has prepared for those who love him" (see 1 Cor. 2:9). So many people today forget that. They picture Heaven as some bright, beautiful place filled with puffy clouds and cartoonish figures of angels wearing long white robes. The images they have in their minds are so unclear and overly spiritualized that it's no wonder they're not more excited by the idea of going there someday.

But that's not at all what Christianity teaches about Heaven. Christianity teaches that if the world we're living in now is real, then Heaven is not going to be less real than that. It's going to be *more* real—more colorful, more dynamic, more adventurous, more creative, more filled with passion, more filled with energy, more filled with relationships, more filled with love.

And after the Resurrection, Heaven isn't just going to be a spiritual place; it's going to be *physical* too. That means that when you see your mother or father or sister or brother or son or daughter again, you won't just be seeing an unrecognizable ghost. You'll be seeing *them*—their whole person—body and soul. You'll be able to run up to your loved ones and hug them and kiss them and look into their eyes and feel the warmth of their skin and talk to them and hear their voice again—the same way you did when they were alive. Only the love you share with them will be deeper than ever before and completely untainted by all the petty jealousies and animosities and grudges that constantly plague our relationships here on earth.

The main thing to grasp is this: If you've lost a relative or a friend and that person is with God, then they're doing just fine. They're okay. They're happier than they've ever been before. In fact, they're doing much better than you and I. All they've really done is moved homes. They've "relocated" to God's home—Heaven—and they're waiting for us to get there too.

Listen, life is ridiculously short. It goes by in the blink of an eye. No matter what age you live to, it's really just a drop of water in the ocean of eternity. If you've lost a child or a teenager, please remember that. Remember that a person who dies young has just gotten something over with that all of us have to go through eventually. Yes, what happened to that young person is terrible and tragic, but at least he or she is done with the toughest part of life—the dying part. We still have to do it. And while having a good time can be a wonderful thing, having it ten times more by living longer doesn't make it any better. The only thing that counts—and I mean the *only* thing—is getting to Heaven. If you die at ten years old in an automobile accident and become a saint in Heaven, then you've had a magnificent life. But if you die at one hundred, rich and powerful in the eyes of the world, but go to Hell, then your life was a miserable, wasted failure. You've got to believe that—not because of any self-help principles, but because it's *true*. You can read hundreds of spiritual books on grieving and suffering, and they're all going to tell you the same thing. They're all going to say that God has a plan that you can't always see—but it's one you always have to trust in. Everything comes down to trust in God.

Can you do that? Can you "let go and let God"?

Can you relinquish all your anxiety to Him and trust that He'll provide you with everything you need in life, in a time and a place and a manner best suited to your own soul? I'm telling you that you're never going to be happy in this world unless you try. There's just too much pain to bear. You can't shoulder it alone. You're not strong enough. No one is. No matter how much money or confidence or knowledge or power you possess, you're still just a little boat being tossed about on the waves of a stormy sea. At some point, those waves are going to come crashing down on you.

When that happens—when the world becomes just too much of a burden for you—there's only one thing to do. You have to give all your fear and dread and doubt and grief and pain to the One who said, "Be of good cheer, I have overcome the world" (John 16:33). When you do that, when you totally abandon yourself to

God's divine will, He will indeed give you a peace that transcends all worldly understanding because it's not from this world. Rather, it's a foretaste of the supreme peace and happiness that God wants you to enjoy forever—in Heaven.

So once and for all, when you're going through terrible anxiety and suffering and grieving, keep your time frame short. Just get through the day. Make the Sign of Cross as many times as you can. Say over and over, "Jesus, I trust in You." Do your best to carry on with all your normal activities, not to fixate on your problems, and to strive to be even more fruitful, more helpful, and more loving to those around you. Try employing some of the spiritual weapons we talked about yesterday. Find a chapel of Eucharistic adoration near you—or just find a Catholic church that's open—and go before the Blessed Sacrament in prayer. Believe me, if you speak to Jesus in person on a regular basis, miracles are going to start happening in your life!

Above all . . .

Don't doubt!

Don't doubt!

Don't doubt!

Action Items

- ✓ This is another very important chapter, because at some point, great suffering comes to everyone. When that happens, it's hard to know what to do, because fear and anxiety tend to paralyze us. Therefore, the most effective thing you can do now is to go back to the beginning of this chapter and glance through each page. Whenever you see a practical step you can take to help get you through a period of intense suffering, write it down, Don't use long sentences. Just jot down all the to-do items you can find and number them. If something painful or scary happens in the future, you'll be able to refer to this list quickly and begin taking effective action.

All You Need Is Love?

We're getting close to the end of this book, so I think it's time we talked about love.

Everyone seems to think that the most important thing you need to be happy in life is love. Isn't that what the millions of love songs and romance novels and poems and movies and TV shows all say? Isn't that the one thing that liberals and conservatives, modernists and traditionalists, atheists and believers, Christians and Jews all agree on?

Back in the 1960s the Beatles sang, "All you need is love." But didn't the Bible say the same thing more than two thousand years ago? Didn't St. Paul say that only three things last forever: faith, hope, and love—and that "the greatest of these is love" (1 Cor. 13:13)? And didn't St. John say that "God is love" (1 John 4:8, 16)?

Well, if popular culture and the Bible agree—and they don't agree on much of anything—that's pretty good evidence that something might be true. And yet if it really is the case that love is all you need to be happy, why does everyone seem to be so unhappy? If everyone knows the right medicine to take, why are they still so sick?

I'll tell you the answer. It's not that the medicine is at fault. The medicine is 100 percent effective. Love *is* all you need. The problem is that the definition everybody is using for the word "love" is incorrect. The problem is that we have our labels screwed up again.

We talked earlier in this book about how using the wrong label on a map might make you go in the wrong direction and end up in the wrong place. But what if you switched labels on medicine bottles? What if you thought you were taking aspirin, but it was really some kind of hallucinogenic drug? What if you thought you were taking the cure for a disease, but it was really poison?

That's exactly what we've done today with love. We've switched labels on the medicine bottle, and people are swallowing all kinds of "pills" that pass for love but are actually quite harmful—especially if taken at the wrong times or in the wrong combinations or in the wrong doses.

Take "infatuation," for example. Many people mistakenly label that "love." And it's understandable. After all, is there any greater feeling in the world than having a crush on someone? Is there anything better than having those fluttering butterflies in your stomach? That ache in your heart? Those obsessive thoughts flying around in your head? If you've ever been lucky enough to feel that way about someone and then have those feelings reciprocated, you know what a special and magical thing it can be.

And yet is infatuation love? Is that really what the Gospels describe as being *equal* to God? Is it even what the Beatles song is about? Is it all you need to be happy? I don't think so. In fact, if you mislabel "infatuation" as "love," you had better be very careful, because at the wrong time and place, that wonderful, beautiful feeling could be highly toxic.

Don't believe me? What happens if you've been married fifteen years and have three kids and you suddenly get infatuated with a coworker? What happens if you further mistake that feeling of infatuation for love? Is there a chance you might do something stupid and wreck your marriage? Is there a chance you might do tremendous damage to your children? Is there a chance you might ruin your career? If you indulge your desires and give in to your feelings, do you really think that qualifies as love, or is it just a sign of immaturity—and selfishness?

Listen, gasoline is a great invention, and it's what your car needs to function well and take you to nice places, but if you ever drink a gallon of it, you'll end up in the hospital really quick. Likewise, infatuation can be a delicious treat to sample if you're not married and if the person you're infatuated with is single and likes you too.

But if that's not the situation, don't go confusing it for love—because a few too many bites of that treat might be enough to give you a case of food poisoning that could wipe you out.

Or take another example: kindness. Many people mistake kindness for love too. Kindness is when you try to alleviate someone else's suffering. After all, nobody likes suffering. We all want to eliminate it forever. It hurts for us to see people in pain—especially if we love them. And yet isn't pain good for us sometimes? Doesn't it help us to grow? Doesn't it help us to mature? Doesn't it even, on occasion, lead us to happiness? And so isn't it sometimes an act of true love to allow or even cause someone to experience a certain amount of pain?

Come on, you know it's true. A few days ago, we talked about spoiled children and how they become that way. There's probably no better example of love that's been mislabeled. When a child cries and screams because he doesn't want to go to the doctor or to the dentist or to school, it's so easy to give in to him. We don't want to see him cry. We want to be kind to him. We want him to laugh and play and give us lots of kisses. But is it really loving for us to do that? What happens to that child if he doesn't go through the pain he's supposed to?

I'll tell you what happens. If he doesn't go to the doctor, he's going to get sicker. If he doesn't go to the dentist, his teeth will rot and fall out. If he doesn't go to school, he's going to stay ignorant and never go anywhere in life. In other words, he's going to experience *real* suffering later on—and it's going to be *your* fault because of your well-meaning but misguided attempt to be kind when you should have been firm.

The point is that kindness, like infatuation, isn't genuine love at all. It's just one aspect of love. Under the wrong circumstances, it can be disastrous to a person.

So what *is* the correct label for love? How can we understand it in a way that will be good for us at all times and in all amounts? This is one of the key questions in life, isn't it? If we answer it correctly, it will really put us on the right road to peace and happiness. And yet this is where I have to warn you that if you embark on a journey to discover love's true meaning, it's going to take you away from the world of pop culture, with all its phony, silly, shallow clichés. It's going to take you far out of your comfort zone and into some very dangerous territory. It's going to take you to a place where your spiritual, emotional, and physical strength will be tested to the limit. In a word, it's going to take you right up to the Cross.

Yes, the Cross—the greatest symbol of love in the universe. The Cross, because that's what love is ultimately about: self-sacrifice, self-denial, and self-giving—even to the point of death.

True love cares about what's best for the *other* person. Not just what feels good to you. Not just what gives you butterflies in your stomach. Not just what gets you sexually aroused. Not just what alleviates pain. True love is so much more than all that. True love suffers. It sacrifices. It gives till it hurts. But if you practice it, you'll find that it really is a cure-all for life's problems. And the reason is that true love is the *substance* of God. It is magnificent and profound and sublime and, truth be told, almost never soft. In fact, it's incredibly hard. So hard that some have even compared it to a rock—a rock very much like the one on which Christ founded His Church.

But in order to understand this kind of love, you first need to understand something else—and it's very important that we don't skip over it. To understand love, you have to understand life too. Both are tied together inextricably, and any attempt to fathom one without the other is doomed to failure.

Of course, everyone nowadays seems to make a big deal over what a "mystery" life is. So many modern philosophers and writers and filmmakers have tried to discover its meaning but have come up short. In fact, their conclusion has been that the search itself is endless and hopeless and even pointless. But guess what? I can tell you all you need to know about the meaning of life in one short sentence:

> For God so loved the world that he gave his only Son, that whoever believes in him should not perish but have eternal life. (John 3:16)

That's it. That's the "secret" of life. It may not spell out the details, but all the main points are there.

First, there is a God. A personal God. And He loves us.

Second, Jesus Christ *is* God—God the Son, God the second Person of the Blessed Trinity, God in human form.

Third, God became a man for one reason: to save us from our sins. Christians believe that God lowered Himself and took on our human nature so that we could be raised up and share in His higher, divine nature. That's what redemption is all about. After the disobedience of our first parents in the Garden of Eden, human beings weren't allowed to enter Heaven. But through a life of total obedience—even to the point of self-sacrifice on the Cross—Christ made up for the Original Sin of our first parents, redeemed our fallen human nature, reconciled us to God, and opened the gates of Heaven to us. Christ's mission was the salvation of the world.

And *our* mission is to enter into and participate in that salvation—to enter into and participate in the life and work of Christ Himself, by imitating Him, by offering ourselves up like Him, by uniting ourselves to His body, and by becoming what C. S. Lewis called "little Christs." That's the meaning and purpose of life on this planet, and nothing else.

Do you see why life and love are so closely connected? Their purpose is exactly the same—to give, to sacrifice, to be Christlike, to be in union with God.

Now, I know that all this might seem a lot to get your mind around. It is. And if this were a book of Christian apologetics, I would probably spend several chapters giving you all the reasons and explanations and arguments why Christians believe what they do. But this isn't a book of Christian apologetics. It's a "how-to" book on transforming your life and finding true happiness. The "proof" for this book isn't in its arguments, but in the *results* you get.

And the results you get from true love are nothing short of miraculous. In fact, they're enough to transform your marriage, your family, your career, and the entire fabric of your existence. But growing in love is an extremely difficult process. It takes time and effort and practice. Like old age, it's not for sissies.

After all, if you want to grow in anything in life, you have to exercise hard, right? "No pain, no gain." If you want your body to get stronger, you have to exercise it by working out. If you want your memory to improve, you have to exercise it by trying to recall things. If you want to get better at playing a musical instrument, you have to exercise by practicing every day.

Well, it's the same with the spiritual life—especially when it comes to love. If you want to grow in it, you have to exercise by *loving more*. You have to exercise by testing your willingness to give, give, and give some more. And that's exactly what God does to us all the time. He pushes us to our limits. He sends us trials that force us to grow. God is the greatest—and toughest—coach in the world. If you ask Him to increase your faith and your love, don't be surprised if He responds by making life very hard for you—at first.

Did you ever hear the story about the great Spanish mystic St. Teresa of Ávila? She was an extremely holy woman and was always praying to God to increase her faith and love. Once she was traveling in the countryside during the winter and got caught in a storm. It was the dead of night and there was lightning and thunder and wind, and her horse and wagon went off the side of the road and dumped her into a ditch full of mud. As she was struggling to climb out in the pouring rain, she couldn't resist looking up at the dark sky and yelling, "Oh, Lord, if this is the way You treat your friends, it's no wonder You have so few of them!"

Do you feel that way sometimes? I know I do. It's natural. But the question is, if God loved Teresa of Ávila, what motive did He have for treating her that way? He knew she was holy. He knew she was "one of His friends." Yet He was so rough on her. Why? The simple reason is that He was answering her prayer. He was giving her the opportunity to work on her faith and her love. He knew that the only way He could help her to become stronger was to challenge her, to push her to her limits, to exercise her.

And if He did it to her, you can be sure He'll do it to you too! So instead of railing at God when He sends you trials, why not just offer them up and get down to the hard work of increasing your love?

Do you ever do that? Do you ever work on improving your capacity to love? Do you work at loving yourself, for instance? Do you take care of your body and your soul by nourishing them properly and by developing your willpower? Or do you just spoil yourself? Do you simply give in to your body every time it calls out for food or rest or comfort or sexual gratification? If you're not practicing self-control and some kind of fasting, you're just becoming a slave to your flesh. And that's not love.

What about your neighbors? Do you work at loving them—starting with your family? Do you love them, even to the point of death? Christ didn't give just part of Himself to the world. He gave every last drop of blood. Do you do that for your spouse and children? Or do you spend a lot of time whining about how difficult you have it and how ungrateful they are?

What about acquaintances and strangers? Do you practice hospitality—even to people you don't like? Remember, loving isn't the same as liking. Liking is purely an emotion. Love isn't. You can dislike people intensely but still be kind to them, pray for them, and sacrifice for them. In fact, the people you dislike most in life are sometimes the ones God expects you to show the greatest love toward.

Here's a tough one: do you love your enemies? Christ commanded us to do that too. Remember, loving your enemies doesn't mean having warm, fuzzy feelings toward those who have harmed you. It means forgiving them, which means wishing them the greatest possible good. It means praying for them. Do you pray for your enemies? If not, then you're not loving that way God wants you to love.

How about charity? Do you give generously, not just out of your surplus but out of your need, like the widow in the Gospel story, whom Jesus praised as a model of self-giving (Luke 21:1–4)? If you're being generous only because you have extra money in the bank, then stop patting yourself on the back. Go back and read that Bible passage now, because you're not practicing generosity the way you're supposed to.

What about your family? Do you give to them? Do you give to your friends? Do you give to the poor? Do you give, give, give, and then keep on giving? Do you give without expecting anything back—not even credit or recognition? I'll tell you something: if you're looking for reciprocation of any kind, then it's no longer true love you're practicing but just another form of selfishness. Yes, you might be accomplishing some good with your charitable gifts, but if you're eagerly waiting for payback, that only makes it a more "refined," "sophisticated" type of selfishness. True love doesn't ever expect to be rewarded in this life. In fact, it's more likely to be ignored, neglected, abandoned, or punished—just as Christ was when He was hanging on the Cross.

What about the souls in Purgatory? Do you practice love toward them? Do you pray for them every single day? So many Catholics forget about this requirement of their Faith. They automatically assume that their loved ones are in Heaven. But we can't ever know that for sure unless the person in question has been canonized. Do you realize that you might have some very close family members and friends who are suffering in Purgatory this very second? Do you understand they might be there for a very long time? Listen, if life on earth lasts seventy or eighty years, why shouldn't our time in Purgatory be at least that long (assuming that time there is somehow measured in a similar way)? Do you know your prayers can help those poor souls and get them into Heaven quicker? I have a hunch that someday, if and when we get to Heaven ourselves, we're going to be greeted by many of our deceased relatives and friends and they're going to ask: "Why did you stop praying for us? We really could have used your help!"

Don't let that happen! Show your love to them *now*, even if they've been gone a very long time.

Finally, what about God Himself? Do you work at loving Him—or do you just give Him lip service? Do you talk to Him every day in prayer? Do you thank Him? Do you praise Him? Do you worship Him—not just at home but in church? Do you try to obey His commandments—not some of them but all of them? When you fall, do you confess your sins and repent? Do you receive Christ's Body and Blood in the sacrament of Holy Communion as often as possible? Do you read the Bible and pray the Rosary so that you can be immersed in His life? Do you make reverent use of the devotions and the sacramentals the Church has given us for the express purpose of helping us to stay close to Him? And when He sends you trials, do you turn tail and run? Do you whimper and moan and shake your fist at the sky and say, "Woe is me"? Or do you instead say, "Lord, *thank You* for counting me worthy to share in a small part of Your Cross. Help me to carry it so I can use it to honor You and give You glory"?

That's true love.

Again, I know that crosses can be hard. And I know they can be even harder when nobody appreciates them. But you have to remember that *God* appreciates them. In fact, God knows that when you carry your crosses faithfully, it's a sign of your love for Him. St. Thérèse of Lisieux taught that you can do the tiniest, most tedious, most insignificant thing in the world, but if you do it for God and if you try to do it perfectly and without complaining, He will look upon it as if it were a great and heroic deed. Do you understand what that means? It means you can be serving french fries at the local fast-food restaurant, and if you say to God: "I hate this work, but I'm doing it for You, Lord," your humble little offering can have more spiritual firepower than the billion-dollar donation of a pride-filled philanthropist. That's because you've turned your cross into a mighty act of love for God.

You have to get it through your head that the Cross isn't something negative—it's something positive. In fact, if you look closely at it, you'll see that it's a huge plus sign. We talked a few days ago about fighting evil. Do you know that the best, most effective spiritual weapon there is to combat evil is redemptive love—love that has been united to the suffering of Christ? When you love so much that it hurts, it puts you at the very pinnacle of spiritual power. It unites you to the source of power itself—Jesus Christ—at the very moment He demonstrated His saving power to humanity.

When you give without limit, you "plug in" to that power source—and it begins to have a transformational effect on everything you do. When you love the people in your family that way—no matter how ungrateful they may be—your family life begins to transform. When you love the people at your work that way—no matter how irritating they may be—your work environment begins to transform. When you practice the kind of love Jesus taught on the Cross, you yourself begin to transform into the best father, mother, husband, wife, son, daughter, friend, employer, or coworker possible.

But talk is cheap. *Talk is cheap!* You don't bring about that kind of radical transformation by singing Beatles songs! You do it with radical action. You do it by praying and working at it every single day of your life. You do it by getting off your butt and helping people who are suffering. You do it by giving every last drop of blood to your family and your friends and your town and your city and your country and your world. You do it by constantly exercising your love, by sacrificing your wants and needs for the sake of others. You do it by uniting yourself to the Cross.

When you live *that* way—as a Christian is really called to live—then yes, it's true, love is all you need.

Action Items

- ✓ It's time to be radically honest with yourself. Answer yes or no to the following questions:

  Do you love yourself as much as you should?

  Do you love your neighbors—including family, friends, strangers, and enemies—as much as you should?

  Do you practice charity as much as you should—especially to the poor?

  Do you love the souls in Purgatory as much as you should?

  Do you love God as much as you should?

- ✓ If you answered no to any of these questions, how might you do better, starting *now*?

Rest, Review, Celebrate

You're almost home! Can you believe it? You've made it through four weeks. Only two more days to go!

By now you know the drill. Today is a day of rest. You should review your notes from the previous week, celebrate your accomplishments, and go to church to thank God for all He is doing to transform your life.

If you like, feel free to read the next chapter *today*. If you do that, the program will be only twenty-nine days instead of thirty, but it might be worth it in order to keep the momentum of this final week going.

This week has been especially important because we've talked about the Eucharist: God's greatest gift to man. Are you ready to receive that gift worthily today? If you are conscious of any serious sins, have you gone to Confession? If not, be sure you do!

Before attending Mass today, it might be a good idea to review Day 24, "The Time Machine." Try to get yourself into the proper mindset to really appreciate the Liturgy of the Church.

We only have one "reading" day left. After that—on Day 30 (or 29 if you skip ahead)—you'll be writing out a code of conduct based on the contents of this book, and you'll be saying a special prayer designed to make sure this program has a lasting impact on your life.

You've done an incredible job so far. Let's finish strong.

See you tomorrow!

All This and Heaven Too!

The moral of this book can be summed up in one line from the Psalms:

> Unless the Lord builds the house, those who build it labor in vain. (127:1)

So many people today try to "build" their own lives and give no heed whatsoever to the kind of life God wants for them. The end result is that we have a world brimming over with unhappy people.

No one ever seems to learn. So many folks are content to spend the precious few years they have on this planet trying to get more money so they can show off. They might not admit it, but that's the truth. They don't want to buy a house they really love; they want one that looks fancier and makes them appear richer. The same goes for their cars and their clothes and their furniture and all the rest of their possessions. It's all about showing off. It's all about status. It's all about becoming a puppet.

How pathetic! The misguided masses that get caught up in the battle over expensive labels and shiny status symbols just don't realize what a waste of time it is. They don't realize what a waste of *life* it is. Whom do they think they're showing off for? Whom are they trying to impress? What's the point? Do they really think that other people look at them and say, "Wow! John's doing great. He's so rich and successful. I admire John." Are they really silly enough to believe that?

The irony is that people aren't thinking about John at all. They're too busy thinking about themselves! And if they did give John and his possessions a passing thought, it would probably be in a disparaging way. That's just how people are—especially today. They don't view their neighbors' accomplishments with charity and humility—they view them in a spirit of competition; they view them enviously.

It's all a big waste of time. It's all a silly rat race. And as someone very wise once said, the outcome of that race doesn't matter much, because even if you win, you're still a rat!

Is that what you want to be in life? A rat?

The same holds true for people who lust for power. So many of them don't realize that their huge ambition to become "important" and "powerful" is really just a manifestation of their huge ego and insecurity complex. Any worldly position, no matter how lofty, is insignificant in the grand scheme of things. Even the job of president of the United States is grossly overrated. Outside of our own country, being president just isn't a big deal. Nobody cares very much how "powerful" he is. In fact, if the president took a leisurely stroll down the Via Veneto in Rome, he wouldn't even need a security detail. Not one Italian would bother looking up from his newspaper and espresso. The truth is that people who run for elective office because they think it's going to make them important are just kidding themselves. Worldly importance is purely a local phenomenon.

Even those rare individuals who achieve great, international fame are usually forgotten within a couple of generations. If you want proof, just take a trip to England, France, or Italy and walk through some of the ancient churches and palaces. You'll see hundreds and even thousands of marble busts of past monarchs. Nobody even knows who these people are today because time has erased and eroded the names that were carved into the stone. And these were the kings of the world! These were the richest, most powerful men and women of their time. They went to their graves certain in the knowledge that they had secured some measure of lasting fame, that they had really done something special for which they would be remembered.

But they were all wrong. Dead wrong. It was just vanity.

Do you get my point? You have to wake up! You have to forget this nightmare you've been living. You have to forget about impressing the people around you. You have to forget about impressing posterity. You have to stop living a life of worthless delusion. It's all a load of horse manure! The only one you have to worry about impressing is God Almighty. The reputation and standing you have in *His* eyes are the only reputation and standing that count. *He's* the only one who can give you happiness in this life and the world to come—and no one else.

Let's take a moment to talk about happiness again. We've mentioned that word so many times in these pages, but we haven't really discussed it at length. Let's do that right now, and let's be *honest* about it.

The truth is that it's possible to be happy in this life, but you can't ever be *perfectly* happy. If you do all the things this book recommends, I'm sure that you'll be *very* happy. I'm sure you'll experience a state of supreme contentment, joy, and tranquility—one that won't ever be disturbed by the ups and downs of life. As the Bible says, it will be so marvelous, it will transcend all understanding. But don't kid yourself. It *still* won't be perfect. It still won't be complete.

That's the bottom line, and we might as well face it once and for all. I don't care what religion you practice, what belief system you adopt, what method of positive thinking you employ, or what personal-development program you follow. None of those things will ever give you perfect happiness. That's because perfect happiness isn't something you can get from any activity or created thing. It certainly isn't something you can get from the pleasures of this world—not even if you have a lifetime of them.

You know this is true! Haven't there been times in your life when you obtained something you thought would make you happy, but when you finally got it, it didn't produce the effect you desired? Maybe you always wanted a trip to Paris, or you always wanted a boat, or you always wanted to get married, or you always wanted to be wealthy. When you finally got those things, they gave you *some* happiness, yes, but none of them made you completely happy. None of them gave you what you were really looking for. That's because pleasures are always greater in the anticipation than they are in the realization.

In fact, having lots of pleasures can even dull your ability to be satisfied. C. S. Lewis said that the whole lesson of his life was that no method of stimulation was of any lasting use. "They're all like drugs," he said. "A stronger dose is needed each time and soon no dose is effective."[11]

That's why the hedonists of the world are such a pitiful lot. They spend their whole lives chasing mirages—false visions of things they think will make them happy but never do. Then, after they've been disappointed for the thousandth time, they get frustrated

[11] Letter to Mrs. Ray Garrett, September 12, 1960, in *The Collected Letters of C. S. Lewis*, vol. 3, *Narnia, Cambridge, and Joy, 1950–1963* (New York: HarperCollins, 2004).

and disillusioned and turn into cynics. They end up becoming the loudest of complainers, blaming everyone and everything for their problems—except themselves. They say things like "It's my wife's fault" or "It's my parents' fault" or "It's my boss's fault" or "It's the president's fault" or "It's the pope's fault"—all because none of those people ever did what they were supposed to do. They never provided perfect happiness.

But who's to blame for that? The Catholic Church has taught for two thousand years that perfect happiness consists in the perfect fulfillment of *every aspect of our being*. That kind of fulfillment comes from God alone, and it's something we'll be able to experience only in Heaven, when we see God face-to-face.

Ultimately, any unhappiness we experience in life isn't due to a lack of fame or fortune or high position. It's due to a lack of something inside *us*. Human beings were created by God with immortal souls, and those souls can't be satisfied by mere earthly pleasures. Fulton Sheen once said that if the sun could speak, it would say it was happy when it was shining, and if a pencil could speak, it would say it was happy when it was writing—because those are the purposes for which they were made.

Well, *we* were made for the purpose of being in full union with God in Heaven, and anything short of that—including the greatest pleasures of this world—is doomed to disappoint us.

What you have to understand is that all the beautiful, good, and true things on earth from which we derive pleasure are just *reflections* of God Himself, who *is* beauty, goodness, and truth. God is the *source* of all those magnificent reflections we see and experience on earth. Sometimes, at very rare moments, we're lucky enough to get a glimpse of what our happiness in Heaven is going to be like—perhaps when we hear a moving piece of music, or when we see a spectacular masterpiece of nature, or when we're in the throes of romantic love, or when we look into the awestruck face of a child who's marveling at some wonder of life that we take for granted, or when we witness some heroic act of courage and self-sacrifice that reminds us of our transcendent human nature. Usually, those experiences are all too fleeting and strike us in such a profound way that they're beyond words. But in reality, those moments are actually a preview of what Heaven is going to be like *all the time.*

That's a marvelous thing to look forward to. And knowing that imperfect happiness is the only kind we're ever going to have on earth isn't necessarily a bad thing either. In fact, it's a blessing. It means you don't have to be disappointed every time a great experience leaves you feeling unfulfilled. It means you don't have to waste your time searching for any utopias that don't exist. It means you can concentrate on what's really important: making sure you get to Heaven at the end of your days, helping others to do the same, and enjoying the gift of life as much as possible now.

But for the last time, you can't sit still and wait for that joy to be given to you! It's just not going to happen. One of the key teachings of Christianity is that if you want anything in life, you have to first work on *yourself*. Despite the failings of the self-improvement industry, it's very true that self-improvement always precedes great accomplishment—and that includes the accomplishment of great happiness.

People are always batting their brains out trying to change their circumstances or change the behavior of the people around them. But that approach rarely works—so why not just forget it altogether? If you want a better family life, work on becoming the best, kindest, strongest family man possible. If you want to rise in your career, work on becoming the best, most valuable employee possible. In other words, if you want to attract people, work on becoming attractive yourself—not just physically but in every way.

Ernest Hemingway said that if you really do good work and grow creatively, other people will be attracted to you, "as surely as migrating birds are drawn at night to a powerful beacon."[12]

Work on becoming a beacon, and you'll be amazed at how many magnificent things in life come your way.

That applies to the spiritual life too. No great person who reformed the world ever started out by trying to reform the world. Such individuals always began by trying to reform themselves. Only after they achieved some level of self-mastery did God use them in a powerful way to effect lasting change. And doesn't that make sense? If God—the Author of life—wants to "write" something important in the history of the world, don't you think He'd prefer to use the best writing instrument possible? Yes, it's true that He sometimes uses sinners to accomplish His will because He can "draw straight lines with crooked pencils," but He always sharpens those pencils very quickly. He always turns great sinners into great saints.

That's the course you have to set for yourself—to become a great saint. And to become a great saint, you have to endeavor to live a life of *maximum integrity in union with God*. That's the key to everything.

Is that difficult to do? Of course it is! There's a very old but true saying: "God is easy to please but hard to satisfy." Sure, God will forgive you your sins if you're sorry. Sure, He'll welcome you into Heaven if you love Him and trust Him and have faith in Him. But if you really want to offer your services to God, if you really want to do His will and participate in His salvation of the world, if you really want to actualize your God-given potential and become a great human being and a great saint, then there's no doubt you're going to have to work hard.

[12] Ernest Hemingway, *A Moveable Feast*.

But I tell you, my friend, it's joyful work. It's work that will finally free you from being a miserable puppet. It's work that will finally bring you the kind of peace you've longed for all your life but have never been able to experience. And it's work you have the power to do.

You just have to change your perspective. You just have to put into practice some of the things we've talked about in this book. You have to remember the connection between your body, mind, and spirit; you have to grow in your relationship with God through prayer and the life of His Church; you have to try to obey all His commandments, and if you fall, you have to get up again and trust in His mercy; when suffering comes, you have to abandon yourself to His will; when making plans, you have to align your goals with the goals He has set for you; when temptations come, you have to use every spiritual weapon at your disposal to fight spiritual evil; and most importantly, every day of your life, you must attempt to exercise true love—not superficial love—toward both God and your neighbor. Those are the things you have to do in order to practice maximum integrity; those are the things you have to do in order to grow in closer union with God—and those are the things that will give you a foretaste of the happiness of Heaven, *right now*.

And it doesn't matter one bit if you've been a "bad" Christian up to this point. It doesn't matter if you've been the worst sinner in the world. You have an immortal, everlasting soul, made in the image and likeness of God. That means you have superhuman power to completely change your life at any moment you decide.

Listen, when Jesus Christ rose from the dead, who was the first person he appeared to? It wasn't St. Peter. It wasn't St. Paul. It wasn't any of the other apostles. It was Mary Magdalene, a former prostitute!

Did you ever realize that? At the most important moment in all of history, God Almighty—the God of life, the God of love, the God of power, the God of creation—chose to appear to a prostitute before revealing Himself to anyone else. Do you think that was an accident? It wasn't. There *are* no accidents in Sacred Scripture. God was making a very specific point. He was saying that you can start out as the greatest sinner in the world and still end up being *first* in the Kingdom of Heaven.

Once and for all, forget about your past! None of that means anything. The only thing that counts is what you do going forward. The only thing that matters is how you live the rest of your life.

And if you try to implement the things we've discussed and happen to screw up—don't worry. Just go back and reread some of the early chapters. Calmly do an about-face and start again. And if you screw up again, about-face again. And again. And again. Keep starting small and building momentum. Keep praying and fasting. That's a strategy that never fails.

Believe me, God is going to respect your perseverance. He's going to keep helping you get back on track until you succeed—even if it takes years.

Most of all, please don't ever be envious of anybody. Don't waste your time with fantasies about how wonderful it would be to switch places with some billionaire or president or king or queen or model or rock star or sports star or movie star. Those are all nice things to be, but they're all beneath you. *Beneath you!*

You've been given the highest, most magnificent vocation there is in life. It's called being a Christian! Live up to that vocation—really live up to it, not just with words but with actions, with every ounce of strength you can muster. I promise that if you do, you'll have all the love, peace, and joy that this life has to offer—and you'll have Heaven too.

God bless you!

Action Items

- ✓ Nothing to do today but think about the journey we've been taking together this past month. Tomorrow we'll be gathering all the things we've learned into one code of conduct, and then sealing it with a special prayer. Today, simply rest, ponder, and pray.

My Code of Conduct

Behold, I make all things new.

—Revelation 21:5

Well, you made it! Thirty days!

Congratulations! I wish I could shake your hand. You've done an incredible job, and you should be proud of yourself for sticking to this program to the end.

There's only one thing left for us to do: summarize this book and prayerfully commit to implementing its principles.

I've taken the liberty of writing out the main points from each chapter and listing them under the heading "My Code of Conduct." You can copy what I've written, or you can put what you've learned into your own words.

If you choose to use my summary, the important thing is to write or type it yourself. Don't just sign it. Writing or typing it will send a message to your brain that you're *serious* about continuing the process of transformation that we've started. As I said at the beginning of the month, taking an active rather than a passive role is the key to making this program work.

I've also composed a special prayer for you to copy out. The purpose of the prayer is to enlist God's help as much as possible in your journey of personal transformation. There are many "healing" prayers and "miracle" prayers that you can find online that promise amazing results. But in reality, there is no prayer in the world that can *guarantee* either a physical healing or a bona fide miracle, because we can't know for sure what is best for our immortal souls. However, there are certain important elements you can include in a prayer to increase your chances of receiving an affirmative answer from God, even to a request for healing or a miracle (e.g., faith, humility, forgiveness, repentance, and so on). I have incorporated all those elements into this prayer.

Once you've written or typed the code of conduct and the special prayer in your notebook or your computer document, the next thing to do is find a church or a Eucharistic adoration chapel that's open and go there today, or at the very latest tomorrow. Remember, the Eucharist is the Body, Blood, Soul, and Divinity of Jesus Christ. If you want to solidify, confirm, and memorialize the results of this thirty-day program, and if you want to ask God to help you accomplish much greater things in the future, you should go to Him and make your request *in person*!

Listen, you've done a fabulous job this month. But now you have to finish strong! The stronger you finish, the greater your chances of making these changes stick, the greater your chances of making even more progress in the days, weeks, months, years, and decades to come. So do these final action items now and do them *perfectly*.

I want you to remember something. No matter how much you change your life for the better, you're still a weak human being. Chances are you will suffer falls and setbacks in the future. That's okay! I can't emphasize enough that you should do this thirty-day program again—perhaps even annually. And you can always reread any chapters that you've found particularly helpful. Even the greatest pianos need to be tuned regularly; otherwise, they go off-key. So don't be too upset if you occasionally fall back into bad habits. Just stop complaining, about-face, and do whatever you have to in order to get back on track!

And one final thing: if you get a chance, drop me a line on my author website (www.anthonydestefano.com) to let me know how you're doing. I might not be able to respond personally, but I'll definitely get a chance to read your comments and messages. This is something that helps *me* in my own daily struggles. If you've profited from this book, don't be afraid to tell me. I need encouragement, too!

Please know that I'm rooting for you, and more importantly, I'm praying for you.

Now get going! This is a big day for you!

Action Items

✓ Write out the following code of conduct in your notebook. I know it's long, but please take the time to do it. Don't sign it just yet. Feel free to put the whole code or any part of it into your own words and add to or subtract from it.

My Code of Conduct

I, ________________, make a solemn promise to myself that, from now on, I will:

- be aware of all the things I am attached to in life—good, bad, or indifferent—remembering that my ultimate happiness and peace of mind rest solely only my relationship with God
- stop complaining about my problems
- attempt to make my public character, private character, and secret character more integrated and also more conformed to the character God has in mind for me
- recognize the connection between my body, my mind, and my spirt, knowing that what I do to one affects the others and always remembering the importance of strengthening my willpower in order to gain greater control over all three
- do an about-face whenever I start engaging in unproductive or sinful behavior, remembering that my past is not my future

- take small steps when first attempting to make progress in any area, in order to take advantage of the principle of momentum
- always remember that self-help is not enough to transform my life—I need God's help as well
- start every morning by thanking God for another day, praying the Our Father and making a Morning Offering
- never go to sleep without reading a little bit of the New Testament
- make an effort to move as much as possible every day, at all costs avoiding a sedentary life
- make myself, my home, and my work environment as clean and organized as possible
- occasionally fast from food for twenty-four hours when I need to hit the "reset" button and interrupt poor or sinful patterns of behavior
- control my tongue, making every effort to eliminate from my speech vulgarity, obscenity, gossip, lying, and other bad habits
- recall the famous sayings, "What is this in light of eternity?" and "Remember, you will die" whenever something unpleasant happens that causes me to become irritated or angry
- make a firm *decision* to believe in God, even when I experience difficulties with my faith, emotionally
- immediately apologize to God and repent anytime I commit a sin; and if it is a serious sin, go to Confession
- always forgive people who wrong me—no matter what they have done—remembering that forgiveness means wishing a person Heaven, and not necessarily liking them or condoning their actions
- trade in expectation for appreciation, thanking God every day for the things I am most grateful for

- squash sinful temptations when they are small and when I have the power to overcome them
- seek professional help to deal with any harmful compulsions or addictions I may develop
- formulate my goals regularly and prayerfully, taking God's will into account and remembering that "you can't hit a target without a bull's-eye"
- try to be the person who adds the most value to every situation
- work on improving myself a little bit every day in at least one area
- regularly read from my Catholic catechism to better learn my Faith and form my conscience
- regularly pray the Rosary
- worthily receive Holy Communion as often as possible— especially during difficult times, remembering the centrality of the Mass in my life
- resolve to use spiritual weapons to fight spiritual battles, including all the powerful forms of prayer given to me by the Church, as well as the practice of periodically fasting not only from food but from things I enjoy doing
- embrace abandonment to God's will whenever I suffer, remembering the prayer "Jesus, I trust in You"
- refer to the list I made on Day 26 of all the things to do whenever I experience intense suffering and grieving
- practice true love (sacrificial, self-giving) toward myself, my family, my friends, my acquaintances, my enemies, my community, and my country as well as toward the souls in Purgatory and toward Almighty God
- remember the moral of this book: "Unless the Lord builds the house, those who build it labor in vain" (Ps. 127:1)

- endeavor to practice maximum integrity all the time
- fulfill my highest purpose: to become a saint by growing in ever-greater union with God
- live up to my true vocation: *to be a Christian*

Date: ______________________________________

Name: ______________________________________

Signature: ___________________________________

✓ Write out the following prayer in your notebook. Do not fill in your name yet. Feel free to put the prayer into your own words.

Transformation Prayer before the Blessed Sacrament

Lord Jesus Christ, You make all things new and are the Spirit of peace in the universe and the source of all physical, emotional, mental, and spiritual healing.

Today, in Your presence, I confirm that I renounce Satan and all his evil works and that I accept You, now and forever, as my Lord and Savior.

Look upon Your servant, ________________, with eyes of mercy. I ask that You strengthen my resolve to live a life worthy of a Christian; a life in union with Your holy will; a life characterized by virtue, selfless love, and fidelity to Your Church, including the frequent reception of her sacraments.

I ask You to remove any obstacles to self-transformation that I may be harboring in my heart. I sincerely repent of all my sins and likewise declare my forgiveness of all who have hurt me in my life. May Your healing hand rest upon me, and may Your life-giving powers flow into every cell of my body and into the depths of my soul, cleansing, calming, inspiring, purifying, and restoring me.

With confident faith, I ask You now to help me live in accordance with the personal code of conduct I have signed today in Your presence; to bestow abundant blessings on me; to make me new again—in body, mind, and spirit; to relieve all my pain, fear, anxiety, and sickness; and to heal me with Your love so that I may be of service in Your Kingdom for years to come in this life and for all eternity in the next.

I entrust this request to You and to the Immaculate Heart of Your Blessed Mother, Mary, as well as to the entire Heavenly court of angels and saints. Amen.

✓ Find a Catholic church or Eucharistic adoration chapel that is open today or tomorrow. Go there with the notebook or tablet that contains this prayer as well as your code of conduct. Sit in front of the tabernacle for an hour and prayerfully read each article in the code of conduct. If you think you can commit to them, sign the document in the presence of the Eucharistic Lord. Then fill in the blank space in the prayer with your name and read that slowly before the Lord as well. When you are finished, sit there for the remainder of the hour and thank Almighty God for everything He has done for you this month, and everything He will continue to do for you in the future.

Then go forth into the light of a new beginning . . . and a new life.